OUTSIDE
LOOKING
IN

GARRY WILLS

OUTSIDE
LOOKING
IN

Adventures of
an Observer

VIKING

VIKING
Published by the Penguin Group
Penguin Group (USA) Inc., 375 Hudson Street,
New York, New York 10014, U.S.A.
Penguin Group (Canada), 90 Eglinton Avenue East, Suite 700,
Toronto, Ontario, Canada M4P 2Y3
(a division of Pearson Penguin Canada Inc.)
Penguin Books Ltd, 80 Strand, London WC2R 0RL, England
Penguin Ireland, 25 St. Stephen's Green, Dublin 2, Ireland
(a division of Penguin Books Ltd)
Penguin Books Australia Ltd, 250 Camberwell Road, Camberwell,
Victoria 3124, Australia (a division of Pearson Australia Group Pty Ltd)
Penguin Books India Pvt Ltd, 11 Community Centre,
Panchsheel Park, New Delhi–110 017, India
Penguin Group (NZ), 67 Apollo Drive, Rosedale, North Shore 0632,
New Zealand (a division of Pearson New Zealand Ltd)
Penguin Books (South Africa) (Pty) Ltd, 24 Sturdee Avenue,
Rosebank, Johannesburg 2196, South Africa

Penguin Books Ltd, Registered Offices: 80 Strand, London WC2R 0RL, England

First published in 2010 by Viking Penguin, a member of Penguin Group (USA) Inc.

1 3 5 7 9 10 8 6 4 2
Copyright © Garry Wills, 2010
All rights reserved

A portion of this book appeared as "Daredevil" in *The Atlantic*.

LIBRARY OF CONGRESS CATALOGING-IN-PUBLICATION DATA
Wills, Garry, 1934–
Outside looking in: adventures of an observer / by Garry Wills.
p. cm.
ISBN 978-0-670-02214-4
1. Wills, Garry, 1934–   2. Wills, Garry, 1934–   —Political and social
views. 3. Journalists—United States—Biography. 4. Historians—
United States—Biography. I. Title.
JC251.W555 2010
973.92092—dc22
[B]   2010005323

Printed in the United States of America
Set in Palatino   Designed by Francesca Belanger

TO NATALIE
(who else?)

Contents

OUTSIDE
LOOKING
IN

Introduction

A Bookworm's Confession

A reviewer of one of my books in the 1960s said that I did not really belong to the intellectual circles of that time. Though I seemed to be educated, I showed no influence from Freud or Marx, Nietzsche or Sartre, the stars of the fashionable intelligentsia. That was true enough. I had, of course, read them, as was expected from a teacher in secular universities. But they had not entered early or deeply into my mental formation, which did set me apart from my contemporaries in the academy. I can understand why that might make me less interesting to readers, less part of the vital currents of my day. But I did not expect to be interesting. My attention was directed elsewhere, and largely to the past.

The earliest influence on me was that of Gilbert Chesterton, the Edwardian journalist, the subject of my first book, and not a usual figure in intellectual circles. Chesterton's heroes became my early heroes: Charles Dickens, Samuel Johnson, John Ruskin, William Cobbett, Robert Louis Stevenson—again, not hot items in the period's literary world. These figures made me a kind of Anglophile, but not a snobbish one. Chesterton was far from elitist. He was a populist, a man who said that democracy is like blowing your nose—you may not do it very well, but you ought to do it yourself. He also said that democracy means that when someone is drowning, your first instinct is not to say that "a Ph.D. is drowning" but that "a man is drowning." And he said that the ordinary person should not be found guilty of a crime but by a jury of fellow ordinary persons.

Some thought that because I began by writing for William Buckley's *National Review,* I must be a conservative. But Buckley denied that. When he asked me, at our first meeting, if I was a conservative, I said, "Is a Distributist a conservative?" He said, "Alas, no." Philip Burnham, a *Commonweal* editor and the brother of Buckley's *National Review* colleague James Burnham, had assured Bill that Distributism was far from the free-market capitalism that Buckley considered the basis of modern conservatism. Distributism was the politics of Chesterton, neither capitalist nor socialist, arguing for the preservation of private property but for its wider distribution. Liberals, on the other hand, would soon be telling me that I could not belong to them either, since they were secularists—my religiosity disqualified me.

Born in 1934, I grew up in the 1940s, when being a Catholic still set one somewhat outside the national mainstream, ready to look inside without going there. I continued being an outsider when I was an academic looking in on journalism, or a journalist looking in on the academy, not joining professional organizations, not attending their meetings. For eighteen years I taught at Johns Hopkins University, and for twenty-five years at Northwestern University, sometimes full-time, sometimes part-time. When teaching part-time I did a fair amount of journalism, mainly for *Esquire* under its brilliant editor, Harold Hayes, or for the *New York Review of Books* under its brilliant editor, Robert Silvers. Throughout, I was a classicist (Yale Ph.D.) observing modern politics, or a political observer looking back at history.

My father thought I was guaranteeing my inability to make a living when I got my doctorate in classical Greek. That, he thought, would make me a perpetual sideliner. He had always feared that my bookworm ways guaranteed that life would pass me by. It bothered him that, when caddying for him as a boy, I carried a book in the golf bag and pulled it out whenever his party was held up by those playing ahead. One summer when I was in grade school, he paid me money (I think five dollars) if I would go a whole week without reading anything. I took the offer, and used the money to buy a new book.

Far from keeping me out from life, books opened door after door, not so much for me to go through the door as to look through. The most important event in my life occurred only because I was reading a book at the time (Henri Bergson's *The Two Sources of Morality and Religion*). In my home as a child, I read books by flashlight under the bedcovers. This so worried my mother that she asked a doctor if I were not ruining my eyes by reading too much. In the Jesuit prep school I attended, I read in the john at night, the only place where lights were kept on. I was devouring Dostoyevsky novels, which my friend Lew Ellingham had pressed on me. I saved weekends for books I especially hoped to savor, beginning them under a favorite tree. One reading feast I was able to indulge when a traveling statue of Our Lady of Fatima came to the school, as part of Catholic prayers for the conversion of Russia. For three days and nights, an around-the-clock vigil was held before the statue, each student kneeling for a half hour. The lights were on everywhere all night, so I plunged into *War and Peace* and read nonstop for three days and three nights, with only short catnaps, until I finished it. Lew told me it was the greatest novel ever written—and he was right. It is still the novel I most often reread (in various translations)—even more than *David Copperfield* or Waugh's *Sword of Honor.*

In summers, when I was not caddying or mowing lawns, I worked as a stock boy in a men's garment store, unpacking shipments, hanging suits, packing purchased items. In spare time at the back of the store, I read in a cheap volume of all Shakespeare's plays (its print so small I could not read it now without a magnifying glass). At lunchtime I would read the book as I walked to a hamburger joint owned by some relatives by marriage, where I would continue reading as I ate. Over several summers, and with some time in the school year, I finished the entire book, not understanding many of the words but marveling at the music. In school I had been assigned to memorize Mark Antony's funeral oration and Shylock's speech. I also had to memorize other poems as punishment for what the Jesuits called "jugs," for misconduct. Some of those poems I can still recite, though I do not even know who wrote them.

As a wordaholic, I was blessed by my schooling—Catholic grade school, high school, college (St. Louis University), and graduate school (Xavier of Cincinnati). That deprived me of scientific training (I am still an ignoramus on that), but it made me grammatical. One of the false ways to praise a classical education is to say that only those who study Latin really learn English grammar. Nonsense. The way to learn grammar is to diagram sentences, as the Dominican sisters of Adrian, Michigan, taught me—subject, verb, object on the principal line, with dependent phrases or clauses, adjectives or adverbs, on ramifying parts of the structure. Now I constantly read in newspapers or hear on television things like "The body of consultants are agreed," though we Catholic kids of that era knew that "body" was on the main line and "of consultants" was on a subsidiary hook under the subject, so "body . . . is" must be proper. We had no problem with "who" or "whom." No problem with "dangling" constructions—we knew just where they fit on the stemma of the sentence as we plotted it. When I went to a Jesuit high school, I learned to diagram Latin and Greek sentences in the same way, but English came first, not vice versa.

My father was right in one way. Reading has made me not so much a participant in life around me as an observer. I have stood to the side of events. I covered many student protests and antiwar demonstrations, and had many marijuana joints passed to me, but never tried one. I never tried tobacco either. I always hated the smell of cigarettes—my father said he would pay me a hundred dollars if I did not smoke till I was twenty-one, and I won that money easily. Alas, he did not follow his own advice—he and my mother were chain smokers. To get out of the smoky house, I early formed the habit of reading while I walked outside.

I covered as a journalist many political campaigns, but never joined one, worked for one, or wrote a politician's speeches (though I was asked to). When I was on Jimmy Carter's campaign plane in 1976, his speechwriter James Fallows asked me if I did not want to see a campaign from within—I answered that one can be an entomologist without becoming a bug. I have been able to look in on places and events where I hardly belonged—jails, police raids, opera singers' backstage dressing rooms, strippers' changing areas, church rectories, Pentagon offices.

I stayed outside looking in. I was thought by some to be on the right wing or the left wing because I was closely observant of people there—I was, for instance, a friend of Karl Hess in both his libertarian right-wing days as a speechwriter for Barry Goldwater and in his anarchist left-wing days as an antiwar protester. But I have mainly been a conventional person, a churchgoer, one whom Lutheran scholar Martin Marty called "incurably Catholic," saying the rosary every day. I have also been incurably (in a term of the time) square—middle-class, never bohemian or avant-garde (no James Joyce or Beckett, just Evelyn Waugh; no Pollock or Rothko, just Tintoretto; no John Cage or Alban Berg, just Verdi). I have been "stodgy" in my children's eyes, puttering around my midwestern neighborhood unrecognized. (I am normally so unnoticeable that I have trouble getting waited on in stores.) Since I was often writing at home, my children's friends asked, "Why doesn't your daddy go to work?" On the other hand, my daughter, when she was a child, said of a lawyer friend of mine, "He must be a professor." Why? her mother asked. "Because he dresses like a bum, like Dad." I remain old-fashioned to this day. I was very slow to come to the computer and the cell phone, and I have never had any traffic with Palm Pilot, BlackBerry, iPhone, personal blog, texting, Twittering, Facebook, YouTube, MySpace, or other modern tools.

I am so square that I have been married for fifty years to one woman, Natalie, the only person with whom I have ever had sex. I agree with Hilaire Belloc: "It is well to have loved one woman from a child." I have been "faithful" in other ways, teaching classes for forty-three years in two long stretches at only two universities, working with only three literary agents over half a century, in a profession where writers jump about frenetically. As someone so colorless, I am not interesting in myself, but I have been able to meet many interesting people and observe fascinating events, partly by being unobtrusive. My wife says that, because I am so unthreatening, dogs and old ladies loved me. Until I became old myself, old ladies did often mother me, and dogs followed me home (sometimes to embarrassing consequences with their owners). This book presents some of the figures, neither dogs nor old ladies, who fascinated, amused, or educated me. Call it the confessions of a conventional bookworm.

1

Reading Greek in Jail

———◆◆◇◆◆———

The 1968 Democratic convention in Chicago was a swirl of action. I ran in the night from police sweeping demonstrators out of Lincoln Park. I stopped only in a doorway to help my friend Wilfrid Sheed, who had to use a cane from his young polio days. Later, I wiped away tears with other people at Grant Park as Mark Lane, a conspiracy theorist on the Kennedy assassination, flopped dramatically on the ground while his own camera crew treated him as a martyr to tear gas. I had known him since he sued me for an article challenging his conspiracy theories. On a later occasion, coming across me in jail, he would urge me to stay there while he defended me as a protester against the Vietnam War.

It was a mad and noisy scene that night in Chicago, but one quiet event was the most riveting for me. I was talking with a friend, the journalist Murray Kempton, at a checkpoint sealing off approaches to the convention center. High wire fences shunted even those with press credentials to another entrance. The comic and activist Dick Gregory was arguing with the police, saying his home was on the other side of the fence. The police said he could come in, but no one else. "But these are my friends," Gregory said, gesturing to all those around, "and I have invited them to my house for dinner." Kempton snapped shut his reporter's notebook and said, "I never turn down an invitation from Dick Gregory." He went through the gate and was instantly arrested—he would write a beautiful piece that night from jail.

I was tempted to follow Kempton, who was a hero to me. But I was determined to be an outsider looking in, not a participant. I would keep to that standard as I covered other antiwar actions in Berkeley and Toronto, at Kent State, and on the Eastern Shore of Maryland. But events caught up with me in 1972. A recent acquaintance called me at my home in Baltimore and said, "You have written about many antiwar demonstrations. Isn't it time to put the rest of your body where your mouth is?" I resisted, saying how feckless most demonstrations turned out to be. He said that this one would be different. Lawyers were drawing up the constitutional grounds of the action. It would be a First Amendment petition for redress of grievance—a demand that Congress recognize the illegitimacy of funding an undeclared war. Some in Congress had agreed to present the petition on the floor, and we would block the entrance to the chamber until it granted our request. I thought of watching Kempton go through the gate in Chicago and shrugged. "I guess it's my turn."

People I respected had already agreed to take part in this action, and they had been joined by a hundred or so others. So I went to Dupont Circle, to the hotel across from the Institute for Policy Studies, where I was a board member. A strategy session was convened there the night before we were to swarm like bees at the door of the House. The session broke into factional disputes over what to do if and when our petition was not met. We could refuse to leave when the Capitol Police tried to clear the entrance. We could resist arrest. We could move away from the door but hover near to chant our protests. The arguments droned in circles, going nowhere.

Joseph Papp, the director of New York's Shakespeare in the Park, said it was pointless to get arrested once our demand was rejected. Besides, he had business back in New York—he could not afford to stay overnight in jail. Others demanded a more determined course. Weary of the back-and-forth, I went into the hotel bar. Eva Coffin followed me—I knew her from Yale, where she had been the wife of the chaplain, William Sloan Coffin. Though divorced from him now, she admired the spirited activist he still was. She said, "We need Bill here now."

It was finally resolved that everyone should do what he or she wanted on the next day. Dr. Benjamin Spock said that nonviolent noncompliance was the best course, and most followed his advice, though some—Gloria Steinem and Marlo Thomas among them—would fade away when told that anyone staying was under arrest.

When we got to the Capitol, Congress members greeted us—Bella Abzug and John Conyers—and said they would offer our petition inside the chamber. We sat down and scroonched ourselves as tightly as we could around the entry, a bottle stopper to block those trying to go in or come out. At one point, Congressman Gerald Ford came to the door to stare at us. Karl Hess, the former Republican who had written speeches for Ford, got up and stepped over bodies to say hello to his old boss. He reminded him of the things they had said against Lyndon Johnson's war, but Ford, who now supported Nixon's war, did not remember such "good old days." Hess, later that night, would tell me in the cell we shared that he was disappointed at Ford for giving him such a cold shoulder.

The rest of us squirmed around for hours, occasionally distracted by Judy Collins as she sang "Amazing Grace." Gawkers circled the huddle. And then the arrests began, polite and recorded on police Polaroids. Down the Capitol steps, into buses, to be delayed endlessly in an underground garage. The women (about thirty) were taken to the women's detention center— including one who would become a very good friend later on, Ida Terkel (wife of the oral historian Studs Terkel). The men (about seventy of us) were driven to the D.C. lockup. Out of the buses. Our names were taken down by a guard who recognized Spock ("Hi, Doc") from other demonstrations. I smiled to see that Joe Papp was among us, despite all his talk the night before against being arrested. Then taken up for fingerprints and mug shots. (I wondered what Richard Avedon would make of his official photograph.) One phone call (mine to my wife, not a lawyer).

Then into the cells—four of us in two-man cells—a bunk bed (two metal trays with no mattresses or pillows or blankets) and a metal john with no seat attachment. Across from our cell, Spock was rolling up his suit jacket for a pillow and sliding under the bottom bunk (he was too tall to fit in one of the trays). In the cell next to ours, someone complained that the john did not work. Spock shouted, "The john in cell 38, you have to kick the button in the wall." Noisy efforts, with no success. "When I say kick it, I mean *kick* it." Noisy success.

Someone was fingering a flute. The actor Howard da Silva shouted that he should give it to someone who knows music. "David" (the composer David Amram), "where are you?" When Amram answered, down the line, da Silva said to pass the flute to him. After some obscure fumblings from Amram, da Silva shouted, "Send it back!" At this point, Mark Lane went from cell to cell. He had signed the petition the previous night but had kept from arrest, and now entered the lockup pretending to be our lawyer. He came to our cell, instructing us not to plead nolo contendere and pay our fine in the morning, but to demand a trial and make a test case against the war, with him as our attorney. None of us were buying from the self-promoting con man. He wanted a big case he could write about.

Later, I would learn what the women's stay was like from Ida. She said that a guard brought them stew in a styrofoam cup and coffee thick as syrup with cream and sugar. The diet-conscious ladies in their cells—who included Felicia Bernstein and Francine du Plessix Gray—shuddered at the sugary mix. Ida explained to them that poor people all drink their coffee that way, since they are starved for nourishment. Judy Collins gave their cells better music than da Silva had been able to coax from Amram.

During the hours of that long night, I talked mainly with one of my cell mates, Karl Hess. We knew each other from being fellows at the Institute for Policy Studies. Hess was known for being Barry Goldwater's speechwriter in the 1964 presidential campaign. Since then, he had gone from being a libertarian to being an anarchist. He refused to pay taxes used for war purposes, and lived on a farm, creating metal sculptures. An autodidact and devourer of books, he asked what was the volume I carried with me through the arrest. It was the Greek New Testament. He asked why I had it. I answered that I read it every day for spiritual sustenance. Besides, "It's the most influential book in Western culture." Yeah, but why Greek?

I said that learning Greek is the most economical intellectual investment one can make. On many things that might interest one—law and politics, philosophy, oratory, history, lyric poetry, epic poetry, drama—there will be constant reference back to the founders of those forms in our civilization. Politics and law will refer to Aristotle on constitutions and balanced government. Philosophy will argue endlessly with Plato. Historians must go back to Herodotus and Thucydides. Students of Virgil or Milton have to gauge their dependence on Homer. Drama harks back to Sophocles or Euripides for tragedy, to Aristophanes or Menander for comedy. Oratory is measured against Demosthenes or Isocrates, lyric poetry against Sappho or Anacreon. The novel begins with Longus and others. It helps, in all these cases, to know something about the originals. He objected that the remains of ancient literature seem exiguous. That is partly true. Only three of the dozens of Greek tragedians survive, and only about 10 percent of their output. But that gives a kind of detective-story interest to their study. To rebuild the social setting for judging them, one must call on the study of papyri, coins, inscriptions, vase paintings, and archaeological ruins. (The only art history course I ever took was a graduate class on Greek vases.) Karl liked the puzzle aspect of this.

In the morning, after the judge arrived, we were allowed to make individual statements before pleading nolo contendere and paying our fine (I had to borrow some money to pay mine). We scrambled for the few cabs outside the lockup. I ended up in one with da Silva and the writer Martin Duberman. The harried Duberman asked us to go first to Union Station, where he had put his luggage in a twenty-four-hour locker (he had not expected to get arrested). The locker held the only copy of his latest book's typescript (this was before computers), and he was terrified at the thought that the time had run out and someone had taken his luggage. Happily, he found the luggage with the book still in it.

We went back to the Dupont Plaza Hotel for breakfast. Da Silva opened the *Washington Post* and found a tiny notice of our arrest. "I've had better reviews, I must admit." The last time he had been in Washington, it had been in Nixon's White House, where he performed his Ben Franklin song from the musical *1776*. We learned from the *New York Times* why Papp had been so urgent to get back to New York—he was being given the state's cultural medal by Governor Nelson Rockefeller. His wife had to take it in his place, and she announced that he could not be there because he was in jail.

A couple of weeks later, much the same group assembled again at the hotel to plan the same protest, this time at the entry to the Senate. As we crammed ourselves to block the way in and out, Karl came over and sat by me: "I hope we end up in the same cell again." I asked why. "I've been studying Greek, and I want to go over verb forms." Unfortunately, we got separated at the fingerprinting stage and did not share a cell that night. While we were talking in the Capitol, Senator Goldwater moseyed up to the bunch of bodies. Someone told him, "Your old speechwriter is in that crowd." Goldwater said, "Really?" He picked his way through the bodies and pulled Karl up on his feet, shaking his hand, to say, "I haven't seen you in ages. Why don't you come visit me?" Karl, by this time booted and bearded and wearing camouflage garb, said, "I'm afraid your staff would be pissed at me." "Well, piss on them. You're my friend." Later, at the Institute for Policy Studies, I asked Karl if Goldwater was always so warm and gracious. "Always. He is the most loyal and truthful politician I have ever met."

Then he told me something from the 1964 campaign. Goldwater had voted against the Civil Rights Act that spring, and some right-wing crazies thought that if they could stir up race conflict in the summer it would show that Goldwater was right in saying that the civil rights movement should not be caved in to. Word of this got to Goldwater and he called in his top staff— Clifton White, Denison Kitchel, Karl, and others—and told them: "You guys know me well. I want you to get word to the troublemakers that if there are race riots this summer I am pulling out of the race." I asked Karl if he thought Goldwater would have done that. "Of course. He gave his word." Politically, Karl could not differ more from Goldwater by this time. But personally he could not have admired him more.

Karl died before he could carry his study of Greek very far. But another political figure was more successful. I met I. F. Stone at Kent State University, just after the National Guard had shot four students. We were there to write about the event. Stone knew that I taught ancient Greek at Johns Hopkins, and he told me that his fondest wish was to read Plato in the original. "When I retire, I am going to study Greek." We got to know each other well at the Institute for Policy Studies, and he repeated his pledge over the years. When the improbable occurred, and he actually did retire from writing *I. F. Stone's Weekly*, he plunged into the study of Greek. He took some courses at American University, and got some coaching from my old teacher at Yale, Bernard Knox, then director of the D.C. Center for Hellenic Studies. Since I was a night person then, and he had always been, he would call me in Baltimore at 2 or 3 a.m. when there was no one up he could turn to for help. He would ask me, for example, to explain a construction that was puzzling him, or seek advice about Aeolic forms in Sappho or Alcaeus.

But then he stopped calling. The next time I saw him in Washington, I went over to greet him, but he turned and walked away. "What's that all about?" I asked Marc Raskin, the Institute's director. "He's mad at you for your Hiss review. He says he'll never talk to you again." I had reviewed Allen Weinstein's book on Alger Hiss, and had agreed with the book's conclusion that Hiss had been a traitor. Stone's brother-in-law, Leonard Boudin, belonged to the law firm that defended Hiss. So in fact I did not hear from Stone for years—until, one night around 3 a.m. the phone rang. Izzy said, "I can't stand it! I just can't get through this passage. I need help." But it was the last call. He had relapsed from his anti-Wills resolve, but he did not mean to make a practice of it. I was left outside again. I was not only on the Nixon enemies list, but on the Hiss enemies list as well.

Another man who knew the relevance of Greek studies was the CIA director William Colby. He was called to testify to the Church Committee on CIA misdeeds. To the horror of many in the Agency, he meant to be honest in revealing illegal actions

carried out by CIA agents, as the charter of the CIA required—
he would be called a traitor for conforming to the law. To brace
himself just before testifying, he went to see an old friend teach
a class at American University. The friend was Bernard Knox of
the Center for Hellenic Studies. The two men had trained together in England to drop behind enemy lines during World
War II and work with resistance forces (which both of them did).
They had stayed in touch over the years, and Colby knew that
Knox was lecturing that day on *Antigone*, the play about a
woman following her conscience despite resistance from her
family and from state officials. Few knew when he testified the
next day that he was drawing inspiration from a Greek source.

It was only later that I learned how Whittaker Chambers, in
the last years of his life, signed up for ancient Greek classes at
Western Maryland College, near his farm (famous for its
pumpkin-repository of Hiss papers). I cannot imagine four
more different persons than Hess, Stone, Colby, and Chambers.
But one thing they did have in common—the Greeks.

2

"They've Killed Dr. King"

---◆◆❌◆◆---

I was soaking in the bathtub, reading a book (as was my wont), when my wife burst in. "They've killed Dr. King," she said in shock. That is the way we Americans react. "They" killed President Kennedy, or his brother Robert, or Malcolm X. This was not a conscious profession of conspiracy theory, just the idea that there was an apparent inevitability to the deaths of these controversial leaders. It was crushing, but it was not entirely unexpected.

I asked Natalie to call the airline while I threw clothes onto my body and into my bag. She got me the last seat for the flight to Memphis out of Baltimore that night. King had been in Memphis supporting a strike by the sanitation workers. On the plane, I saw Bill Coffin, the liberal activist and Yale chaplain. Once I had stayed overnight at his rectory after I interviewed him in New Haven, and on the plane we shared our horror over what had happened in Memphis. Since Coffin was a famous preacher, I asked if he would speak at any memorial for Dr. King. He shrugged: "If they ask me."

Arrived in Memphis, I dropped my bag at a hotel and went to the murder site (the Lorraine Motel), where I met Art Shay, the brilliant *Life* photographer. He invited me to go with him in his rented car to the police station, to find out what was happening. On our way there, we saw a liquor store whose glass front was broken in. Shay rushed to photograph the ravaged interior while I, always the outsider, stayed on the street to see if more trouble was on its way. At the police station we were told that Dr. King's body had been moved from the police morgue to the Lewis Funeral Home for embalming. We drove there through streets emptied by the curfew.

When we reach the funeral home, there is only one other reporter there. We huddle in the main viewing room to talk with the owner, Clarence Lewis. On the other side of a thin partition, he tells us, is the operating room, where morticians are at work on Dr. King's body. We can hear the black radio station playing King speeches while his speechless body is being repaired. "His jaw was shot away," Lewis tells us. "We have to build a plaster jaw and powder it dark."

When at last they bring the body out, at 8 a.m., there is a scrim over the open coffin. Shay protests that he cannot photograph through a scrim. Lewis agrees to take it off. "People would probably just tear it off to see him anyway." A line of mourners (all black) had formed outside at dawn. When the crowd is let in, Lewis stands poised to intervene if anyone tries to touch the makeup on the artificial jaw—one woman does kiss the cheek, and Lewis quickly guides her away. Shay later sent me a picture of the first grieving women who filed past the coffin—it hangs over my desk as I write this.

We hear over the radio that Dr. King's widow, Coretta Scott King, is about to arrive at the airport, so we drive there. She was slow to come, since Jesse Jackson, who called her with the sad news, wanted to soften it by saying simply that her husband had been shot, not that he was dead. She had gone to the airport in Atlanta to fly to the husband she thought was injured. But Mayor Ivan Allen gave her the full news of her husband's death before she boarded the plane. At that, she turned around and went back home to steady her children. Now, the next day, she is about to reach Memphis. The plane must be emptied onto the tarmac, with Mrs. King coming down a rolling stairway. Shay grabs another stairway and pushes it close to the one that will be used. He climbs on it to have a good angle for seeing her as she emerges. But the police rush out to clear Shay off the tarmac. He tries again with another rolling perch, but they stop him again. He will have to use a long-distance lens.

After Mrs. King comes in, Shay follows her motorcade back to the funeral home, while I go to the union building where meetings of the sanitation strikers have been held. Inside, a large crowd has come to hear preacher after preacher mourn and memorialize Dr. King. Given the emotional occasion, there is a good deal of weeping, as over a dozen Baptist ministers preach call-and-response sermons. "Dr. King was *for us*," the preachers call out, and the congregation shouts, "*Tell* it! *That* he was." I go over to Bill Coffin and ask again if he means to say something. "Not here," he answers; "this is the *big* league." The crowd and the speakers are perfectly united in grief and in biblical resources, as wave after wave of "*Stay* there!" rumbles from the congregation.

The best speech is the last. In fact, it is the most moving speech I have heard, then or now. The preacher is a compact and natty black minister, with oddly precise diction and smoldering eyes, James Bevel. He has been a prolific inventor of strategies for King's Southern Christian Leadership Conference, some strategies brilliant, some crackpot, all of them daring. He was in the forefront of the sit-ins, the freedom rides, Freedom Summer, the opposition to the Vietnam War. He was the one who persuaded King to include children in the march at Birmingham in 1963, and he helped pressure the Johnson administration into the 1964 Civil Rights Act by threatening to march children from Birmingham all the way to Washington. He had been married to the beautiful and brilliant civil rights leader Diane Nash, for a time his even braver (and saner) better half.

At the union hall, Bevel begins quietly, matter-of-fact: "Dr. King died on the case. Anyone who does not support the sanitation workers' strike is not on the case. You getting me?" They murmur that they are. "There's a false rumor around that our leader is dead. Our leader is not dead." They shout, but tentatively, "No!" Does he mean his spirit is not dead? "That's a false rumor." More support, but wavering: "False!" He is picking up the rhythm: "Martin Luther King is not"—not *dead,* they seem to anticipate—"Martin Luther King is not *our leader.*" Stunned, they hesitate and wonder. "Our leader is the man"—what man? the whole company is caught up in suspense—"is the man who led Moses out of Egypt." Now they know, and they cry *yes* with relief.

Our leader is the man who went with Daniel into the lions' den. Our leader is the man who walked on water in Palestine. He is the man who came out of the grave on Easter morning. Our leader never sleeps or slumbers. He cannot be put in jail. He has never lost a war yet. Our leader is still on the case. Our leader is not dead. One of his prophets died. We will not stop because of that. Our staff is not a funeral staff. We have friends who are undertakers. We do business. We stay on the case, where our leader is.

After each sentence there is a high sobbing response. He has touched just the right chords for that day and that place.

Bevel speaks to an even larger crowd the next day, and speaks well, but not with the magic of the moment in that first speech. After this second sermon, I go up and ask Bevel for an interview. He brushes past me, saying he has no time for that; he has to get ready for the funeral in Atlanta. Mrs. King is conferring with Ralph Abernathy, Jesse Jackson, and others. They are preparing for a memorial march in Memphis before going to Atlanta for the burial (Robert Kennedy has chartered a plane to take them there). The SCLC leadership seems to be neglecting the sanitation strikers. The union spokesman, a rotund little garbageman named T. O. Jones, tells me that SCLC leaders promised to arrange for a fleet of buses to take them to the funeral in Atlanta, but T.O. has trouble confirming the arrangements. A hundred and fifty or so are supposed to gather at Clayborn Temple, the unofficial headquarters of the strike, on Monday, April 8, bringing their best clothes to wear at the funeral when they reach Atlanta.

But at nightfall, long after the buses were to be there, none have come. Some white clergymen, able to move around in the curfew, manage to scout up three buses—not enough for the crowd. The only way to fit everybody into the three is to take folding chairs from the church and line them up in the bus aisles as the regular seats are filled in. A person must take a chair with him or her to the back and sit in it, followed by another person with a chair, carrying it and sitting, leaving minimal space for knees and feet. I ask if one journalist can be fitted in, and T.O. assures me I can. They welcome the only white person in their midst.

The trip was long—ten hours—but it passed quickly in joint musings, hymn singing, and laments for King. To get to Atlanta, the buses had to dip down into Mississippi, then cut across Alabama, going on into Georgia. When a man said we were now in Mississippi, a woman moaned, "Oh no."

T.O. worried what would happen in Mississippi if some white hotheads saw 150 blacks debouching from buses in the middle of the night. He decided that rest stops should take place in isolated places, where unwelcome company was least to be expected. The buses could not stop at gas stations with restrooms. There were restrooms in the back of only two buses. The aisles of those two had to be cleared, while men used the john in one and women used that in the other. Then the chairs had to be replaced, one by one. Some men naturally tried to go behind a tree to relieve themselves, but T.O. did not want them exposed singly to any passersby, and he herded them back to the johns on board.

The strikers and their wives arrived in Atlanta, rumpled and tired, on Tuesday morning, too late to file by the casket that lay in state at Spelman College, or for the funeral service held at Ebenezer Church. They had no time or place to change into their good clothes. Two men rushed the wreath they had brought, a tribute from the strikers, over to the church. The rest watched on the street the funeral procession to South View Cemetery. The casket was carried on a wooden farm cart drawn by mules, followed by a huge procession filled with dignitaries, including some of that year's presidential candidates: Richard Nixon, Robert Kennedy, John Lindsay, and Hubert Humphrey. The burial over, the strikers and their wives went back to their buses for the ten-hour return trip to Memphis.

After Dr. King's death the SCLC people had to complete the Poor People's Campaign he had begun. They lobbied in Washington for the Economic Bill of Rights. Bevel was active in this effort, and he decided to make Washington his headquarters when it ended. While he was there, someone brought to his attention what by then I had written in *Esquire* about his great Memphis speech. He called me in Baltimore and invited me to come see him in Washington. I said I was busy at the time, so he asked to come visit my home. I said I would be glad to see him. He arrived in his neatly tailored coat with a cape over it, hugged me, beamed: "Brother Garry!" Hugged my wife: "Sister Natalie!" I hung up the coat and cloak in the closet, then he got on the case.

He was founding a new organization, MAN, an acronym for Making a Nation. He was planning a one-man march from Washington to the UN building in New York, to demand that a separate black nation be created in America. He wanted me to accompany him on the march as he stopped at various cities to speak. I was to record his exploits in a book. He would give me 10 percent of the royalties. I said I had other writing projects I

25

could not interrupt. He protested, "You owe it to the movement. It needs you. Your talent should be dedicated to this great cause." He was good with words, and a seductive demagogue. But I still resisted, and he said he would give me 50 percent of the book's profits. No. Finally, he said I could keep all the proceeds—this would be his own donation to the cause. When it became clear that he was not going to get his way, without a word he got up, went to the closet, took his coat and cloak, and left. No good-bye. No Brother Garry. No Sister Natalie.

It was the last I ever saw of him, but I heard of him over subsequent years as he grew more weird and exotic. He became a Republican congressional candidate in 1984, and the vice-presidential candidate of Lyndon LaRouche's party in 1992. In 2007, three of his daughters, who had been sexually molested by him in their youth, decided his youngest daughter should be protected from him. (He admitted at this time that he had sired sixteen children from seven women.) One daughter let Virginia police record a phone call as he admitted that he had had intercourse with her and administered a vaginal douche afterward. That was enough to convict him of incest in 2008. There is no statute of limitations for incest in Virginia, and it took the jury only three hours to convict him. The judge fined him fifty thousand dollars and sentenced him to fifteen years in prison, though he died of cancer while trying to mount an appeal.

My experience with other men who worked with Dr. King was far happier than my brush with Bevel. I especially came to admire Andrew Young and Jesse Jackson, who were initially less important to the SCLC than Bevel but were ultimately more solid in support of Dr. King's goals. Once, when I went to visit

Young during his time as mayor of Atlanta, the black cabdriver taking me to City Hall said, "I don't like that place. Just about all the people there are preachers—or lay deacons, which is worse." I said that these were preachers who had gone to jail. "That's the trouble. They're trying to put everyone else in jail, just because they went." When I repeated this conversation to Young, he laughed and said the man was almost right—he reeled off the names of all his aides and appointees who were veterans of the SCLC or other civil rights ministries. I asked about the claim that he wanted to put other people in jail. He explained that the cabdrivers were angry at him for new restrictions on rapacious drivers or those ignorant of the city.

Young came to the civil rights movement as a comparative outsider, but he turned that position into an advantage. Like Obama after him, he was accused of not being black enough. Other SCLC leaders were Baptists; Young is a Congregationalist, trained in the North (at Connecticut's Hartford Seminary). Others, like Bevel, Ralph Abernathy, and Hosea Williams, had rural and hardscrabble childhoods in the Cotton South. Young was the son of a prosperous dentist in cosmopolitan New Orleans. His father had white as well as black patients, and some patients (like Louis Armstrong) were celebrities. Both of Young's parents were college graduates, and he was mocked by other blacks in grade school for being too snooty and middle-class. Young told me that his mother and father were not interested in black culture—a thing one might have guessed from the fact that they named him Andrew Jackson Young after the white president.

Young originally became a minister with the goal of doing

missionary work in Angola, as one of his pastor mentors had done, but by the time he was ready to go there the Angolan government was banning Christian missionaries. Young went to work for the National Council of Churches in New York, running youth outreach projects. From there he wrote to Dr. King (whom he had not yet met) asking for advice on contributing to the civil rights movement. When he flew into Tennessee to join in a voter-registration drive, he arrived in a chartered plane. The down-to-earth organizer Septima Clark let him know this was no way to join dirt-poor people getting literacy qualifications in order to vote.

Young would continue to have problems being accepted by people like Hosea Williams, but King knew exactly how to use Young's quasi-outsider status. Williams would mock Young for going to jail so infrequently (only three times), but King wanted him outside when King was inside. They became the Blanchard and Davis of the movement, "Mr. Inside and Mr. Outside." (Doc Blanchard and Glenn Davis, both Heisman Trophy winners on the same West Point football team, made thirty-eight touchdowns between them, Blanchard plunging through the line as Mr. Inside, Davis sweeping around the end as Mr. Outside.) King wanted Young to be outside negotiating with authorities and publicizing what he was doing in jail. Young told me that he tried to keep sheriffs and the FBI informed of the SCLC's plans, to prevent violent reactions to surprise. His diplomatic role made Hosea Williams charge him with being an FBI plant—and the needling finally brought the nonviolent Young to fisticuffs.

I went back to Atlanta in 1990 to report on Young's race for governor. He had been re-elected twice as mayor of Atlanta (the second time with 80 percent of the vote), but in a statewide race for governor he was having trouble with the white rural areas of Georgia. Taking no security detail with him, he drove me around the city in his own car, pointing out projects for which he had brought in funding, the Underground Atlanta stores he had brought back. He took me to Jimmy Carter's presidential library. Young had worked mightily to bring the summer Olympics to Atlanta, but the Olympics board had not yet announced its decision by Georgia's election day. If it had, Young might have beat Zell Miller in the gubernatorial race, but he was losing when I talked with him.

I asked Young why he had reversed his earlier stance against capital punishment, though his daughter remained a passionate activist against execution. I had just come from covering Dianne Feinstein's campaign for governor in California. She too had changed her views on capital punishment, after having opposed it while serving on the state's parole board. I asked her why she switched her stand. She said she had read recent studies that proved capital punishment is in fact a deterrent to crime. I said I had read much of the recent material that reached an opposite conclusion. Which studies was she referring to? She said she could not remember them, but would send me their titles (she never did). Had Young become convinced that executions are a deterrent? No, he said; but the anger of his police officers who caught murderers and saw them get life sentences, with the possibility of parole, made him feel he had to recognize their feelings, for the sake of their morale. The price Mario Cuomo had paid in New York for his principled opposition to the death penalty had been studied by others running for governor in their states.

Though Young never became governor, his services to Dr. King will live in history, and his implementation of President Carter's human rights policies while Young was the ambassador to the UN was a kind of late fulfillment in Africa of his early longing to go to Angola.

I came to know Jesse Jackson better than Andrew Young. Jackson, in fact, asked me twice to ghostwrite his memoirs. He had the contract for a book, and Frank Watkins, the man who ghostwrote his newspaper columns, had drafted a proposal, but the publisher was displeased with it. Memoirs by veterans of the civil rights movement were a touchy subject. Young refused to write one—his book was about the goals of the movement. Young would not even talk with Taylor Branch while he was writing the first volume of his great biography of Dr. King— only after he saw how profound was Branch's respect in the first volume did he cooperate on the next two volumes.

The civil rights movement, occurring in the turbulent sixties, with young people carried away by passion and the fear of death, had some scandals that people wanted to hide. After Ralph Abernathy's book referred in a gingerly way to Dr. King's sexual affairs, Coretta King froze him out of the King community. Bevel's weirder antics were even more embarrassing. And in a homophobic time, Bayard Rustin's gay life, though well known to journalists and others, was not explicitly mentioned for a long time. There were also jealousies and backbiting, like that between Hosea Williams and Young or between Bevel and Jesse Jackson.

I followed Jackson in his first quest for president, in 1984, beginning with his "exploratory" trips, when I was the only journalist with him on commercial airline flights. He went back to schools that he had visited at a time after Dr. King's death, when the civil rights movement seemed to have faded away. One teacher told me she always welcomed him back, since students were more earnest, at least for a while, after he gave them his pep talks on black achievement. "They did their homework, they wanted better grades." Jackson told the students they had to better themselves, no one else would do it for them. There were some years in the seventies when his was the only voice these students would hear from a civil rights leader.

That became clear when, on the floor of the 1984 Democratic convention in San Francisco, Andrew Young was booed by some black delegates. Leaders called an emergency black caucus meeting to repair the damage done to their solidarity. But when Coretta King rose to demand an apology to Young, she was booed also. Young slipped away, out the back of the stage. A young black delegate standing next to me shouted at Mrs. King, "That was yesterday. What have you done for us today?" A panicky call went out to Jesse Jackson. When he arrived, he stormed onto the stage next to Mrs. King and gave the assembled young delegates a tongue-lashing. "How dare you show disrespect to this woman, whose husband was killed, whose children were threatened, working for the rights of blacks?" After he had silenced the flashy young delegates, he called many onto the stage to lock arms and sing "We Shall Overcome." No other leader had, at that time, the credentials with young blacks to pull off that act of reconciliation.

I saw Jackson's approach to the young when I went with him, during that exploratory campaign, to see his son Jesse Jr. play football at St. Albans prep school in the District of Columbia. Jackson was up and down the sidelines cheering his son on, and Jesse Jr. ran well, but not well enough for his team to win. The other side had an even better black runner. At the end of the game, Jackson raced over to the other side to talk with the young star. "You're a great runner. What's your time in the hundred-yard dash?" "Oh, I don't know," he answered, "but I'm fast." "What about the grades?" "Not so good." "Well, you know, there will be a time when you aren't so fast anymore. Then you'll wish you had studied more, to be good in other ways." The boy said he would try. As we walked away, Jackson chortled to me, "Don't you love it? *'I'm fast.'*" He was taking great pride in the kid's pride.

Jackson impressed on his own son the need for study. When Jesse Jr. entered Congress, he took his oath of office in Spanish. When a journalist asked him why, the new representative said, "My father told me he was embarrassed to travel the world and be unable to speak any language but English. He had studied French in college, but not enough to command the language. He made me promise I would learn at least one other language." I remembered the teacher who had told me her students studied harder after Jackson warmed up her classroom with the chant "I *am—somebody!*" The country is full of people who stood a little taller in their youth because of Jesse Jackson.

3

Dallas

————◆◆✕◆◆————

Ovid Demaris said that he never saw me looking more out of place than when I sat on the floor of a stripper's changing room, under a rack of scanty clothes, while "Tami True" came offstage and threw a robe over her pasties. We were soon joined by Bill Willis, who had been underlining Tami's bumps and grinds with his drums. Tami pouted that Bill "takes limits," which meant he forgot his rhythms while composing plays in his head. We were in Barney Weinstein's Theater Lounge, one of the rivals to Jack Ruby's Carousel strip joint, and Weinstein had inherited Tami and Bill, with other entertainers, after the police closed the Carousel. These Carousel veterans loved to tell Jack Ruby stories—he was a clumsy but lovable clown in their eyes. He was too impulsive and undisciplined to be a trustworthy member of any conspiracy.

Bill Willis, a bodybuilder who won the title Mr. Texas, was supposed to be a bouncer as well as the club's drummer, but he said that Jack often got to a troublemaker and threw him out before Bill could get off the stage and do the job. Ruby cultivated the police, haunted their headquarters, taking them coffee, giving them free tickets to his club. He often carried a gun because he took the money from the club to the bank every day. My friend Ovid, who was in Dallas writing about organized crime at the time of the assassination of Kennedy, had stood around for hours waiting for Oswald to be brought out into the police garage. He told me there was no way to know exactly when that would happen, and Ruby—who had run some ordinary errands just before—happened to come into the garage when Oswald appeared. None of those who knew Ruby thought he was capable of a deliberate plan. He just reacted as he did when throwing a troublemaker out of the Carousel.

Ovid and I were in Dallas in 1966 because Harold Hayes, the brilliant editor of *Esquire* in its glory days of the sixties, sent us there to write about Ruby. Ovid was a former police reporter who knew Dallas well. Hayes admired his ability to get interviews with elusive characters but did not think he wrote very well. Hayes believed that if anyone could arrange an interview with Ruby, it was Ovid. Hayes's plan was that Ovid would set up an interview with Ruby and I would conduct the interview and write it up. None of us knew, when this article was conceived, that Ruby was about to be diagnosed with terminal cancer and the authorities would cut off all access to him.

I was still teaching Greek at Johns Hopkins, so the interview was supposed to be arranged for my Christmas break. Ovid had spent several weeks lining up his old contacts in Dallas. It soon became clear to him that we would not get to Ruby, but he did not want to tell Hayes that, since he was collecting a vast body of material—from a colorful cast of people who had known Ruby: from the Dallas establishment; from the city's strip-joint underworld; from those who had participated in Ruby's arrest and trial. He felt that, if I agreed with him, he could justify the project in ways that Hayes had not envisaged. I went to Dallas from Baltimore at the beginning of my extended Christmas break (Hopkins had a "minimester" before the resumption of regular classes). This was the first Christmas I would be away from my family. (The next one would also be caused by Hayes.) Ovid sat me down to hear tapes he had made with the district attorney and city prosecutor, with some of Ruby's defense attorneys, with a motley assortment of businessmen (including Stanley Marcus), with strippers, police pals of Ruby, and others. Though Ovid had not got to Ruby, he seemed to have set up cordial relations with everybody who had anything to do with Ruby's club life and shady acquaintances. He suggested I go see any of these people I thought promising for an article.

I called Harold to see if he wanted an article of this sort. He did. When I turned in the article, it had just reached the point where Ruby was shooting Oswald. Harold told me to do another article to get Ruby through his arrest and trial. For this second article, I interviewed the prosecutors and defense attorneys in Dallas. Then, back in Baltimore, I read the trial transcript and all the volumes of the Warren Commission testimony on Kennedy's assassination. When Tom Wolfe assembled an anthology of articles for his book *The New Journalism*, he wanted to include my account of the Ruby trial. But he showed me his introduction, where he said that, for the New Journalist, it was "all-important to *be there* when dramatic scenes took place, to get the dialogue, the gestures, the facial expression, the details of the environment."[1] I pointed out that I was not at Ruby's trial. He thought from the vividness of my account that I must have been. When he learned I was not, he included instead my account of Memphis after the shooting of Dr. King, where I had been present.

Bill Alexander, the bright and sadistic prosecutor of Ruby, took great delight in tormenting Ruby's main defense lawyer, Melvin Belli, the so-called King of Torts, whose San Francisco office pioneered medical-claims cases. Belli was so used to handling medical testimony that he began to think of himself as a doctor. For his Dallas case he claimed that the flickering lights in the garage where Oswald was shot had triggered an epileptic fit in Ruby. He went through great rolls of encephalograms with the jury. Alexander asked Belli's expert witness on radiology if all things do not give off radiation. The man said yes. Even the railing around the jury? Yes. Even the wall of the courtroom? Yes. Alexander was delighted to hear from the police guard that when the jury went into its deliberation room that day, some of its members rushed over to the wall and put their ears to it, trying to hear the radiation.

Alexander knew how to get Belli's goat. He called the girdled man "Mr. Belly." When Belli complained to the judge that the prosecutor was mocking him, Alexander sardonically pronounced his name Mr. Bell-EYE. The short Belli wore shoes with uplift heels, which Alexander, talking with reporters, referred to as "fruit boots." Joe Tonahill, the Texas attorney Belli recruited as his local colleague for the trial, told me that "Mel was at his wit's end over Bill's treatment of him." Tonahill was a study in himself. He had a wheezy Christmas cold and cough when I interviewed him in a coffee shop. Since he had brought no handkerchief with him, he first blew his nose on the paper napkins at the table, then on the doilies placed under our coffee cups, then on the little paper envelopes holding sugar for the coffee, leaving a soggy pile of these materials on the floor beside his chair.

When the Ruby articles appeared, an editor at New American Library asked me to expand them into a book. But others were not pleased with them. I was threatened with three lawsuits. The first one was silly. I had quoted Ruby's cleaning lady in a way that suggested he was not planning any great act on the fatal day. A Dallas lawyer, perhaps wanting to discredit exculpatory evidence on Ruby's part, asked the cleaning lady if she had given me an interview. When she said no, he wrote *Esquire* to say he was suing me on her behalf. Actually, I had taken her words from the Warren Commission volumes. She had not only said exactly what I quoted, but had said it under oath when testifying before the commission.

The second suit was pursued further, into the deposition-taking stage, and it was filed by Mel Belli, who claimed that I had defamed him. Everything I had said about him I had on tape, was in the trial record, or was from the Warren testimony. *Esquire*'s lawyer asked if I had further derogatory material that I had not used, to prove that I was not just throwing any old charges at him. I said yes. I had got from another of Belli's lawyers a letter written to the Texas bar by Ruby's sister, who was supposed to be Belli's employer. She complained that he would never report to her, or even see her. He was always too busy. Finally, she went to Belli's hotel during an afternoon break in the trial, knocked on his door, and was admitted on the assumption that she was picking up the room service trays. She found Belli in a circle of reporters, including the famous Dorothy Kilgallen. He was stripped to his jockey shorts, and was taking butter patties from the room service, putting them on a bread knife, and flipping them up to stick on the ceiling. The lawyer said Belli would never go to trial, where that letter could be introduced.

The third suit came from another lawyer, Mark Lane, the conspiracy theorist who claimed that Ruby was part of a plot to cover up the assassination of President Kennedy by removing any possibility that Oswald could talk of it. One of Lane's arguments was based on the testimony of a woman to the Warren Commission. Though her testimony was included in the voluminous record, it was not even referred to in the report written as a summary of the commission's findings. For Lane, that was a proof that the Warren Commission was also party to a cover-up.

The name of this woman was given by Lane as Nancy Perrin Rich. Her testimony was of a type familiar in the long line of witnesses before the Warren Commission. In her thirties, she had been everywhere and known everyone. She once worked for King Faisal of Saudi Arabia. She had been an FBI informer. She was married to a man who had run guns into Spain for Francisco Franco. She had worked as a bartender in Jack Ruby's club but left when he roughed her up; when she tried to file charges against him, the police protected him.

She next saw Ruby at a meeting with a military officer where her husband was asked to run guns into Cuba as he had into Spain. Ruby showed up at this meeting, glared at her, and went into an inner room. At another meeting with the same people Ruby also appeared—but so did the son of organized crime lord Vito Genovese. She recognized him from a picture, not of him but of his father. This was a little hard even for Lane to swallow, so he fudged her testimony, saying simply, "A person was present whom Mrs. Rich thought she recognized as someone associated with syndicated crime."[2] This testimony convinced Lane that Ruby was connected with military, pro-Castro, and mob plots. He attacked the Warren Commission for not following up on the testimony, talking to all the people Mrs. Rich identified (though she had often forgotten their names). And he was suing me for defamation, since I had ridiculed his charges.

Because I had read all the Warren volumes, I knew not only that the Rich testimony was internally inconsistent but that it did not match similar stories told by two other witnesses. Lane should have cited these as corroborating the Rich story, since—despite differences—much of what was alleged in the other two places resembles what Rich was saying. There was a good reason Lane had to neglect those two tales after rebuking the Warren people for neglecting Rich's evidence. The reason is that the two other witnesses were Nancy Perrin Rich under two different names. Ovid, with his tracking skills, found Rich's husband, and I asked him if he had talked with Lane. He said yes. Did Lane know about the other two times she testified before the commission? Yes. Why did she tell three different stories under three different names? Because she was mentally disturbed. She was under treatment when I called the husband. Lane knew all these things and did his own cover-up in order to accuse others of cover-up. I told all this to *Esquire*'s lawyer, and asked why Lane would bring a suit when he knew all these things about the Rich story, and that they would come out at trial. The lawyer said it was a nuisance threat, meant to intimidate me and make me stop talking about him.

The Lane case brings out a problem with all the conspirato-rialists who fish around in the many volumes compiled by the Warren Commission, finding "evidence" that the commission did not use in the report. The commission was open to anyone who felt he or she could contribute to its knowledge. It sup-pressed nobody's testimony. But it did not knock down each false allegation. It did not, for instance, embarrass the poor dis-turbed woman Lane exploited by showing that she babbled three different accounts, all equally and wildly implausible. There were many nuts, fanatics, and obsessed people who vol-unteered to speak to the commission. I know this because I was acquainted with one of the fanatics, Revilo Oliver.

Oliver was a very learned classicist at the University of Illi-nois, whom I met on Bill Buckley's yacht before Buckley stopped using him as a book reviewer because of his growing anti-Semitism. After that, Oliver helped found the John Birch Society and wrote ever more extreme stuff. He not only thought fluo-ride in the drinking water was a Communist effort to poison Americans—he foiled the plot by keeping a water cooler in his front room full of unfluoridated water, to drink himself and to serve to his guests. Oliver told the Warren Commission that the International Communist Conspiracy had trained Oswald in Russia and dispatched him to kill Kennedy, "who was doing so much for it," because "the job was not being done on schedule."

He rejected the idea that Communists had killed Kennedy "because he was planning to turn American." On the contrary, he said, he saw no evidence that Kennedy planned to "turn American." Instead, the assassination of Kennedy was meant to trigger the backlash killing of true patriots all across the land. That plan failed only because the Dallas police captured Oswald. Then the Communists had to send Ruby to kill Oswald before he could reveal the plan.

Eventually, Oliver became too crazy even for the Birch Society, and he was forced out, making his few followers call him a martyr, "the man who knew too much." The Warren Commission did not publicly refute Oliver any more than it did Rich. It did not want to spend decades chasing down the phantoms of fanatics. But that left it vulnerable to men like Lane who could use the fanatics to create their own phantoms.

NOTES

1. Tom Wolfe and E. W. Johnson, *The New Journalism* (Harper & Row, 1973), p. 21.

2. Mark Lane, *Rush to Judgment: A Critique of the Warren Commission's Inquiry into the Murder of President John F. Kennedy, Officer J. D. Tippit, and Lee Harvey Oswald* (Holt, Rinehart & Winston, 1966), p. 295.

4

Turbulent Times

———◆◆◆◆◆———

After earlier urban riots—Watts, Detroit, Newark—there
was great fear that the cities could succumb to a general
conflagration in 1968. Political and police leaders went into a
flurry of preparations for trouble, buying armored vehicles and
testing new technologies for crowd control. The Pentagon did
studies on better ways to back up National Guard units, as it
had (belatedly) in the Detroit riot. The Institute for Defense
Analysis (IDA) studied the range of nonlethal weapons that
could be used on citizens (exotic things like "liquid banana
peel"). The FBI issued a manual, *Prevention and Control of Mobs
and Riots.* The President's Commission on Law Enforcement and
Administration of Justice made riots a new focus. Antiwar demonstrations were increasing and authorities were scurrying
about to cope with the threat.

In this climate, *Esquire*'s editor, Harold Hayes, sent me to
nine cities to talk with mayors and police officials on what preparations they were making for control of the threat. I flew over
Watts in a police helicopter. I toured Chicago in police cars. I
talked with the police chief in Detroit, Ray Girardin, who said
the riot there would not have been so bad if Governor George
Romney had not wanted to promote his presidential race by

refusing federal troops for too long. I talked to Frank Rizzo, the tough police commissioner in Philadelphia, who had heavily armed teams cruising around the clock for quick response to trouble. Rizzo had new weaponry, including a Stoner gun that could shoot snipers not just at a window or on a rooftop but by firing through a brick wall at them. In Detroit, a police official took me to a range to fire a Stoner gun and showed me a block of clay that had been hit. I could put my fist through the hole— imagine what that would do to a human chest.

A Pentagon adviser told me that the IDA report was bumbling. If I wanted to learn about nonlethal weapons I should go to the young genius who had invented Mace, Alan Litman. I went to Litman's home for an afternoon and evening, eating dinner with him and his wife. Litman was an experimental designer fascinated by the principles of structure. He had patents for a whole range of new products, not just for Mace. As a college student, he had done experiments on the intelligence of sea life, and he still had, in basement tanks, the crocodile (smart and tamable) and alligator (dumb and dangerous) he used in the experiments. He liked the design principles evolution had given them. Of his crocodile, whom he called Ernst, he said, while tickling the sack under his jaw:

He's a masterpiece of design. See this ridge? It curls the water off around his eyes so he can get up speed without blinding himself. And this bunch of muscles here protects the hinges of his jaw. His teeth are all askew, you notice—he drops and replaces them constantly. He has an inner thin lid under his heavy eyelid—it slides side-

ways, he can see through it, and it corrects for underwater refraction of light so he can strike accurately
underwater. Ernst is a great fisherman.

To demonstrate the inadequacies of the IDA report on nonlethal weapons, he took me out on his porch and fired some
of them. Tear gas drifted back on its user unless he was half
blinded with a mask. He smeared a little pepper spray on my
cheek. In twelve minutes it had begun to sting. Twenty minutes
later it had left a red irritation. "It's a great deterrent for a man
attacking you, if you can manage to run away from him for
twelve minutes." Why does pepper spray work on dogs?

It gets into the nostrils and mouth, and on the tongue,
and has a good chance of getting in his eyes. But with a
human, the nostrils and mouth are dry and not so accessible. To be effective on a human, you have to score a direct hit in the eyes—which are easily shielded or simply
closed. For some reason, the Institute of Defense Analysis has shown an entirely disproportionate interest in
pepper.

I asked how he had invented Mace. After a friend of his wife
was mugged, he experimented with the deterrents available to
his wife. They were either ineffective or dangerous (not really
nonlethal). He needed something that could be directed in an
aim-focused stream that would disable without permanent
harm. He found the right combination of chemicals, and he and
his wife took out the patent. Some civil rights groups claimed

the effectiveness of Mace showed it had lasting harmful effects. To disprove this, the chief of the Cook County police in Illinois, Joe Woods (brother to Rose Mary Woods, Richard Nixon's secretary who handled his tapes), had himself shot with Mace on TV.

Litman said one need not go that far to do an experiment on oneself. He squirted some Mace into the bathtub and told me to duck my face down for a moment near the wet spot—even in that mild dose, it made me feel like my face was on fire. Mace was not for sale at the time except to police and military units, but Litman gave me several bottles—and for years my wife kept one by her bed when I was traveling out of town. Litman stopped giving interviews about his invention as it caused more controversy, so law review treatments of its toxicity had to cite Litman from my *Esquire* article as the main source on its safety.

In Chicago, I was driven around for two days by Hutch and Duke—James Hutchinson and Leonard Hunter—two deputy sheriffs hired by Joe Woods to be his Youth Council. They were black policemen in their twenties, Vietnam veterans, who spouted statistics like sociologists and analyzed the various communities, black and white, they drove me through. They were black militants, but they controlled the young men like themselves by saying, "Don't be stupid." Their heroes were men like Stokely Carmichael. "He never lied to us." They had no respect for most of the Chicago police, but they liked Woods, who never condescended to them. They had more intelligent things to say about riots and riot control than I had heard from most policemen or politicians.

After I had completed my tour of nine cities, I went to the

Pentagon to interview the provost marshal general, Carl Turner, the commander of military police, on his preparations for urban disorder. Turner was in charge of troops at the March on the Pentagon, which had not been handled well (I was there to see that). But he admitted no error, nor any uncertainty in his role of "making doctrine" (as he put it) on riot control. When I asked to interview him, as the man responsible for riot response, he refused, saying the press had no right to know what the military was planning: "I have too often been the screwee from the press." When I went above him and got a Pentagon official to say he must respond to legitimate questions, he received me with great and surly hostility.

I asked permission to tape our interview and he refused. I said that it was a protection for him, against misquotation. He answered, "If the newsmen are going to misquote me, then I say to hell with them." He brought with him two public relations people from the Pentagon, who throughout the interview regularly reduced his answers to euphemism or placation, to his obvious disgust. When he got to "making doctrine" over riots, he told me that the first priority, when trouble impends, is for the police to take all the guns from gun shops. When I ran this idea by various police chiefs, they snorted with derision. Apart from the legal problem of seizing property in this way, the diversion of manpower to the task would take officers away from dealing with crowds, just when they are most overstretched.

Turner's second idea was to handle snipers in a building by driving an armored car up to the building and debouching teams inside to hunt the snipers from within. When I said that most police forces did not have armored cars (yet), he said that you can hang armor on a truck. My impression, which I conveyed in the article, was that General Turner was a ninny. This so infuriated J. Edgar Hoover, when the article was brought to his attention, that he had me investigated. I would not learn this for several years, but the point is that he sent an agent to talk to General Turner and get his refutation of my *opinion*. I had not committed any crime. This was part of the FBI's thought control. But though I had committed no malfeasance, Turner did. He was forced to resign as chief U.S. marshal when it was discovered that he sold 688 weapons confiscated from rioters for his own personal gain, without reporting his profit to the IRS. (No wonder he wanted police to seize guns wholesale.)

My next experience of the turbulent years was in Knoxville, Tennessee. In 1970, President Nixon was having trouble going anywhere in public without burdening the local police with control of violent protests against his appearance. He solved that problem in the spring of 1970 by going to a sympathetic area (Knoxville) to enter a locally patriotic venue (the football stadium of the University of Tennessee Volunteers) where a religious rally was scheduled by one of his most popular supporters, the preacher Billy Graham. Any protest there would be not only a disturbance of the peace but an interruption of a religious service, which is against the law in Tennessee. (Police handed out copies of the relevant law at the entrance to the stadium.) No placards would be admitted to the event. Young protesters folded up large sheets of paper with the Bible quote "Thou shalt not kill." But when they took them out and held them up, they were hustled out and arrested. Some shouting protesters were arrested later, identified by police photographs of the event.

I had met with young people planning to protest the rally. They were liberals and radicals in a conservative enclave. They had not been very successful activists. One confessed that he flunked Arson 101. He had tried to burn down the ROTC building. After putting gasoline-soaked rags all around the wooden structure, he lit a fuse across the street and waited to watch the empty building go up in flames. But he had bought a slow fuse, one that crept along for an hour and then fizzled. I kept in touch with these feisty people after I left Knoxville, since they told me what was happening to those arrested at and after the Graham crusade. Then, one day, one of them called me from Canada. He and others had fled the draft and were living in a commune with other war protesters (some deserters from the army). They invited me to visit them, and I did. I listened to their stories, ate their frugal meals, played touch football with them.

When I left, I suggested they call me with any developments in their touchy relationship with the Canadian authorities. They said they could do so only if I left my credit card number with them. That was a mistake. My wife, who pays the bills, soon noticed that a number of calls were going from Canada to other parts of America—apparently the commune members were calling their family and friends on my dollar. But they did not put any other purchases on the card. They were honorable in that respect.

My wife was also noticing odd sounds on our telephone. She had asked several times that I get any FBI files on me that might exist. She thought the FBI might be tracking the deserters and activists in Canada. I thought it more likely that they would be interested in my ties with the Institute for Policy Studies. When the IPS got its files, they ran to thousands of pages. The FBI had planted an agent in the Institute, posing as a secretary. He rummaged through the refuse of the offices, looking for incriminating papers. He even took used typewriter ribbons to the Bureau, so its lab could reconstitute typed messages. One of the Institute directors, Dick Barnet, liked to get out of the office and walk around Dupont Circle for fresh air. When a visitor wanted to talk, he would suggest they do so while strolling. The FBI plant said that was when crimes were discussed, and the agency should track anyone who went outside with Dick.

One of the fellows at the Institute with whom I became friendly was Ivanhoe Donaldson, a handsome man from the Caribbean who had been a charismatic firebrand in the civil rights movement. Our relationship got off to a shaky start. He denounced me the first time we met as a collaborator in the extermination of black leaders. *What?* He said that *Esquire* had done one of its customary charts on leading figures in any field. This one rated the most influential blacks in America. They were arranged in concentric circles around an inner core. Since this gave the chart the appearance of a bull's-eye target, Ivanhoe said it was an invitation to shoot at the people being rated.

I learned that Ivanhoe liked to set people back with challenge on a first meeting. But if you stood up to his bluff, he opened up to you—as he did to me. One night in Washington we went to visit another black leader, who was throwing a party for visiting Africans. One of the guests, a white woman from South Africa, got the Ivanhoe treatment. He denounced her for South Africa's racial policies. She was foolish enough to say that the policies, though wrong, were understandable. A tense argument followed, which culminated in Ivanhoe's slapping her. The host went into his bedroom and came out with a pistol, telling Ivanhoe to get out of his apartment. Ivanhoe whispered to me that he could talk the man down, but I should go wait for him in the reception hall of the apartment building. I did so. Shortly after, Ivanhoe came down smiling. I asked if he had smoothed things over. He said, "Of course." He was a charmer.

It was late, and I said I had better get my car for a return to Baltimore. He assured me, "No need," and invited me to stay with him in an apartment he was using. It turned out to be a large and lavish apartment loaned him by a rich backer who was out of town—Ivanhoe had a gift for cultivating wealthy patrons. Later, he became an adviser to Washington mayor Marion Barry, access to whom Ivanhoe used to line his pockets. When the police caught on to what was happening, Ivanhoe was convicted and sent to jail.

Though I had resisted the idea of requesting FBI files, since others had told me that it is a cumbrous process—you have to prove that you are you and then you have to wait for all the legal reviews and redactions to take place—I thought that by now I had enough radical acquaintances that J. Edgar Hoover might have some record of them. But when I got my files, seventy-two pages of what are called "Bufiles," I learned that the Bureau was ignorant of what was really questionable. Hoover was interested in nothing but my views. The Bureau put extra and useless energy into thought-police activity rather than crime control.

Hoover began his scrutiny of me because of the interview with General Carl Turner. Because of the *Esquire* article, he asked that an agent go see Turner. Since the general was in Europe at the time, the agent could talk with only one of the public relations people who had sat in on my interview. The PR man said that I was hostile (it was Turner who had bristled at the very idea of the interview) and that I was "sensational" and "twisted the truth." The only factual point the Pentagon challenged was that I said the FBI manual on riots had been written by a military man. The PR rep said that, in fact, a military man had been heavily drawn on and quoted in the manual, though he had not written the whole of it.

Okay, why was it "sensational" to claim that he had? I had not said that this made the manual less important or less true. It was not relevant to the main point I made about the interview: that Turner's claim that seizing guns and using armored cars in sniper control was the basic "doctrine" of riot control. On that the Pentagon said nothing. Nonetheless, when several people—journalists and Hoover acolytes (their names crossed out in the files released to me)—wrote to J. Edgar Hoover asking if he "had anything" on Garry Wills, he answered that the Bureau had made an investigation and found that I was "sensational" and "twisted the truth," quoting the public relations person as if that were the result of a Bureau investigation.

But the thing that most upset the Bureau was a newspaper column I wrote when a congressional investigation turned up the facts about the "COINTELPRO" (counterintelligence program) operation of the FBI. Hoover himself wrote a letter protesting my column to the head of the syndicate that distributed my column. That person, John McMeel, sensibly ignored the protest. What I referred to was the way the FBI tried to foment violence between the Black Panthers and other radical black organizations in Chicago and San Diego—faking letters of vituperation between them, sending forged insulting cartoons, and making anonymous phone calls. The Bureau argued in internal documents that it was trying to *prevent* violence by making it impossible for these activist groups to cooperate.

It could not be preventing violence when one of the forged letters, sent to Chicago's Blackstone Rangers leader Jeff Fort, ostensibly from a black sympathizer, said: "The Panthers blame you for blocking their thing and there's supposed to be a hit out for you. . . . I know what I'd do if I was you." The latter invitation to murder was like the invitation to suicide in the FBI's famous anonymous letter to Dr. King. The same files that brought me Hoover's letter saying I was egregious in suggesting that the Bureau was fomenting violence brought me the confirming documents that proved that it was. God bless the Freedom of Information Act.

In 1972, I got a phone call in Baltimore from a man saying he had a message for me from my Chicago police friends, Hutch and Duke. It was too important to discuss on the telephone. Could I meet him in Washington? I went to the hotel he named as our meeting place. When I got there, he said he had rented a room: we could not talk in a public area. We had to wait for an empty elevator to go up to the room—he refused to get on one with other people. When we got there, he patted me down to make sure I had no gun. Then he pulled the shades down, went to the bed in the corner, sat on it, edged himself back into the corner ("I always keep my back to a wall"), pulled out a pistol, and laid it on the bed beside him.

I was surprised when I met this fellow, since he was white,

and Hutch and Duke had told me there were few whites other than Joe Woods that they would ever trust. But the man assured me he was a constant adviser to my friends—in fact, he knew all the black leaders (including "the two Big Jims," James Farmer and James Bevel)—and was a full-time protector of the civil rights movement. Indeed, he was forming an elite paramilitary troop to step in when riots occurred, to keep police from mowing down the blacks. He wanted me to be the chronicler of his efforts—it was Jim Bevel time all over again. But this man was even crazier. He held me for three hours spinning his fantasies of power. He claimed that Nelson Rockefeller would be the patron of his squad, and that this would make Rockefeller president. He and I would prove to be kingmakers. Every time I tried to get up and leave, he put his hand on his gun—now I knew too much about his plans for him to let me go until I joined the cause. At last, promising to give his ideas the most careful thought, I got free. Luckily, I never heard from him again. I did not call on Hutch or Duke to see if they were buying this man's nonsense. I did not have the heart to do it, since I feared they might be. In all the odd things I witnessed during those turbulent years, this was the oddest. Like Bevel, this man dismissed me when he could not bully me into his scheme.

5

Baltimore

When my wife and I moved to Baltimore, for me to teach at Johns Hopkins, I continued to be an outsider, a journalist in the academy and a professor in journalism, but it was the second most settled time of my life (I would spend even more time at Northwestern). The only real Baltimore insiders in the family were our children. Two of our three came there as pre-schoolers, and the third was born there. Each acquired a Baltimore accent as a toddler, which shows how powerful is peer influence. They did not hear Baltimore sounds from their parents, or from the radio or TV. It was their playmates they wanted to imitate. So they said "speeyoon" for spoon, "meeyoon" for moon, "telephayown" for telephone. They had the Tidewater diphthongs. They shed these mannerisms only when they went away to college, where they imitated different peers.

Tommy Three

One of the great Baltimore institutions I observed was Thomas D'Alesandro III—Tommy Three as he was known—the mayor in the late sixties. Now I suppose he is most famous as the brother of Nancy Pelosi. She is often attacked as a San Francisco liberal; but I knew her as a Baltimore Italian political pro. I met her when she came back to town for the vote count on election nights, a family tradition. She and Tommy Three are the children of Thomas D'Alesandro Jr., the former Maryland congressman and Baltimore mayor.

Tommy Three is a wonderfully down-to-earth person, unpretentious and funny. He loves to tell stories against himself. He recounted for me once how he went to a political dinner in Pennsylvania and asked the man sitting next to him what he did for a living. "I'm a painter." Since it was winter, Tommy said, "Isn't that seasonal work?" He soon found out it was not seasonal work for Andrew Wyeth.

I served with Tommy on an ecumenical education board, and found out how useful it can be to have a good politician as one's partner. We had to deal with a founder of one seminary program, a man who had aged beyond his ability to keep his own project working. We wanted to ease him out, but he did not want to go. Tommy said there was no problem. Just invent a new title for him, give him several awards, and flatter him to the sidelines. He had the fulsome skills to make that strategy work—and it did.

But Tommy could also be blunt. In this, he resembled his father, Tommy Jr. When journalists were pestering "Big Tommy" (as he was known), one reporter said, "My desk needs an answer to this *right away*." Tommy Jr. held up his hand, leaned over, put his ear down on his own desk, lifted his head, and said, "*My* desk tells *your* desk to go to hell."

When Dr. King was killed, Tommy Three had the gruesome

task, as mayor, of riding around the city in an armored vehicle during the riots that followed on that tragedy. It deeply disturbed him: "This is not the Baltimore I grew up in." He decided in the aftermath of his own turmoil that he no longer wanted to stay in politics. But when he said he would not run for re-election as mayor, so great is the assumption that those in power cannot relinquish it that rumors of ethnic scandal were whispered to explain his retirement: "You know these Italians. There must be some Mafia tie involved in this." Tommy laughed things off, but the rumors persisted. So he called in the City Hall reporters and said, according to what he told me, something like this:

I've heard what they are saying about my not running again. I want to give you the real story. I have not told it to anyone but you. This is a nice job. Every morning I get up and there is a limousine waiting outside my house, heated in winter, cooled in summer. I get in and there is a newspaper for me, and a cup of coffee. I arrive here and everyone is nice to me as I come in—"Hello, Mr. Mayor. How are you, Mr. Mayor?" I come into my office and sit down behind this big desk, and my secretary comes in with a big silver tray. It is piled high with shit, and she asks, "Will you please eat this, Mr. Mayor?" It takes all day, but I get it down by the time I have to leave. And the next day she has another tray ready. Why should I want to keep doing this?

The TV series *The Wire*, based on Baltimore politics and created by a reporter from the *Baltimore Sun*, had its fictional former mayor tell something like this story, but this is the version I heard from Tommy's own lips in my own house.

When Jerry Brown first ran for president in 1976, he won the Maryland primary and was flying high. I went back to California with him on his plane, and he thought his victory had set him on the road to the White House. I later learned from Tommy why he actually won there. The state's governor, Marvin Mandel, was under federal investigation and would shortly be going to jail, but he could still muster his machine's forces—they turned out for Brown, since Mandel hated the other primary candidate, Jimmy Carter, with whom Mandel had clashed at governors' conferences. Nancy Pelosi had known Governor Brown in California, and she introduced him to Tommy, who showed him around town. After one event, Brown got back into the limousine and beamed a question at Tommy. "What do you think, Mr. Mayor?" Tommy replied, "I think you're a prick, Mr. Governor." Why? "Those people on the dais with you worked all night getting this thing together. But you didn't pay tribute to a single one, mention a single name, shake a single hand." Tommy said he had been deliberately harsh, to shake Brown out of his bad habits. But Brown kept up the same behavior in the following meetings. Finally, driving him to his last evening rally, Tommy said: "Do me a favor. Don't mention anyone's name or shake anyone's hand. I'll just say it's our campaign strategy."

Nancy Pelosi has the same needling humor as her brother. I saw her soon after the death of Robert Drinan, the lawyer-priest and antiwar activist who served in Congress until Pope John Paul II ordered him to leave political office. She spoke at the funeral Mass for Father Drinan, and noted that the pope had clearly played a providential role. When Drinan stepped down, the voters put in his place the openly gay congressman Barney Frank.

Jonah House

Another Baltimore institution I wrote about as an outsider was Jonah House, the religious commune founded by the ex-priest Philip Berrigan and the ex-nun Elizabeth McAlister, which campaigns against nuclear weapons. Phil had become famous in 1968 when he and his brother Daniel, a Jesuit priest, were two of the "Catonsville Nine," antiwar activists who broke into a draft headquarters in Catonsville, Maryland, and defaced draft cards with blood before burning the cards. Phil and Liz made more headlines in 1972, when President Nixon's attorney general, John Mitchell, tried to convict them and five others of planning to kidnap Henry Kissinger. I covered this trial of the "Harrisburg Seven" in Harrisburg, Pennsylvania, for *Harper's*. It was there I first met Alger Hiss, who came to speak in favor of the Seven. The jury did not believe the charges against Berrigan and the others. They went free. It was Mitchell who later ended up in prison, for his Watergate crimes.

Jonah House survives, though Phil is now dead. I reported on many communes in the 1960s and 1970s, in college towns and in Canada. They were all short-lived. Only Jonah House has gone on and on, still recruiting young people for demonstrations and writing campaigns that argue no one has the right to make and maintain weapons that can destroy much or all of the human race. Jonah House was named for the biblical figure who lived in the belly of the whale, which is how the Berrigans saw Americans living in the national security state that was fostering the deadly nuclear system. Every year, on the liturgical feast of the Holy Innocents—those children slaughtered by Herod when Jesus was born—the Jonah House people would go to the Air and Space Museum in Washington and sing hymns around the model of the Hiroshima bomb. I went with them, and wrote about their eloquent arguments against nuclear fantasies of power.

Phil and Liz rotated the kinds of protests at nuclear sites that led to their being imprisoned. One would stay out of jail while the other went in, so the outsider could bring up their children, who became antiwar activists in their turn. Though Jonah House received some donations from peace activists, it supported itself for years by doing manual tasks, especially house painting. This was not only an economic necessity but a statement of solidarity with the working class. There are many homes in Baltimore that have a careful coat of paint put on by some of the most famous jailbirds in America.

I did not lose touch with the Berrigans when I moved from Baltimore to Evanston, Illinois. There I went to church with new friends, Dick and Nancy Cusack. Dick had been Phil's college roommate at Holy Cross, and they were antiwar activists themselves, as were their actor children. Nancy was arrested while protesting the work of the School of the Americas, which trained enforcement figures for South American dictators. I dined with the Cusacks whenever Daniel came to visit (Phil was too often in prison to come west).

When Daniel had gone underground to avoid arrest, and led the FBI a merry chase, J. Edgar Hoover's agents went to the Cusacks to see if he had been in touch with them. When their young daughter Annie came in from school, the agents asked if they could question her. Nancy said, "Sure." Annie asked what this was all about. Nancy told her, "These men are looking for Father Dan." Why? "They think Father Dan has done something wrong." "That can't be. Father Dan wouldn't do anything wrong."

When Phil died in 2002, the Cusacks' actor son, John, who could not leave the set of a movie he was making, lent his parents the private plane he uses. I went with them back to the city made holy by Jonah House, where I renewed acquaintance with its members. Phil was buried in a plain wood casket, and Daniel preached an eloquent sermon based on the raising of Lazarus. In the plane on the way back, Dick told me his story of the pope's beanie. He and a Holy Cross classmate, on graduation, went to Rome and attended a Mass at Saint Peter's. The pope at the time was Pius XII, who came into the basilica carried on men's shoulders in the *sedia gestatoria*. It was his practice to throw his white skullcap (the zucchetto) into the crowd as he passed. Dick and his friend scrambled for the prize, and had equal rights to it, so they agreed to rotate possession of it when they went home. But when it was Dick's turn to have it, he loaned it to his mother, who started passing it around to friends to cure their various ailments. He never got it back. (I dedicated my book on the rosary to Dick, though he was not much of a rosary sayer in his last years.)

John Waters

A quite different Baltimore institution was the moviemaker John Waters. He was just beginning his weird career when we moved there—filming on the streets of his hometown with amateur equipment and friends as his only actors. I went to his "world premieres" at midnight in a local theater after the regular runs were over for the day. He brought a red carpet and searchlight to the events. His "stars" entered through thin ranks of fans. The first movie I saw, in 1968, was *Eat Your Makeup*. Despite his "underground" fantasies, and compliant actors who did stunts like eating a dog turd for the camera, he came, later in his career, to make more conventional films—like *Hairspray*, which led to the lavishly remunerative Broadway version of the story.

But there is nothing conventional about the Christmas cards he still sends out every year, cheerfully ghoulish creations. He claims that the first card he created was a conventional Joseph-Mary-Jesus crib scene on which he replaced the baby Jesus's face with that of Charles Manson. I did not see that one, but I did see the card that re-enacted his police mug shot (from a time when he was arrested for restaging the Kennedy assassination on a Baltimore street)—he made it a Christmas card by putting a Santa hat on his photographed image. Another year, his "card" was a clear plastic Christmas-tree ball, with red lettering on the outside that said "Merry Christmas from John Waters"—inside, on its back, little legs in the air, was a dead cockroach. One of my sons has a collection of all the cards John sent us. It is one of his most prized possessions.

Knowing John helped me in 1973. I was part of the crowd at a counterinaugural protest at the beginning of Nixon's second term. The police dispersed us with tear gas and chased us from the midtown area. As we fled, we tried to evade the police by streaming into an underground garage, a poor tactical decision, since they trapped us there and brought up a bus to put us in after arrest. John was there with his camera crew, filming for background scenes in his next movie. There was a TV camera crew there, and perhaps the police thought John and his actress, Cookie Mueller, were with it. (They were better dressed than the rest of us.) At any rate, when the police tried to push me onto the bus and I showed them my *Esquire* press pass, they paid no attention until John came over and said, "That's all right. He's with us." I went free, vouched for with the police by the auteur of *Pink Flamingos*, the dog shit epic.

Unitas and Berry

We were in Baltimore during the glory days of the Baltimore Colts football team—a team full of stars: John Unitas, Raymond Berry, Lenny Moore, Alan "the Horse" Ameche, L. G. Dupre, Gino Marchetti, John Mackey, Artie Donovan, Eugene "Big Daddy" Lipscomb, Jim Mutscheller, Alex Hawkins, Jimmy Orr, Lenny Lyles. I had not been a Colts fan before we moved to Baltimore in 1961. In fact, I was rooting for the other side when the Colts won their first national championship (1958), in what is widely considered the greatest football game ever played, against the New York Giants. I was dating my future wife at the time, in her hometown of Wallingford, Connecticut, and I watched Giant games with her father, John Cavallo, rooting for Frank Gifford, Sam Huff, and the other New York players.

I could not watch the championship game with John, since it occurred over the Christmas break and I was visiting my parents in Michigan. I heard the first part of the game on my car radio, but when it went into late minutes with the Giants ahead, I ducked into a bar to watch on television. Then, though the whole Giants defense was keying on the wide receiver Raymond Berry, Unitas hit him with three passes in a row, taking the ball into field goal range. That kick tied the game and sent it into overtime. Unitas steered his team to victory in the first overtime ever played in professional football.

In Baltimore, my whole family succumbed to the town's fascination with the Colts. And as the sixties turned to the seventies, and the team cooled off, we were close to two informal shrines to the Colts, since we lived just a couple of blocks away from Unitas's restaurant (The Golden Arm) in one direction, and Artie Donovan's liquor store in the opposite direction. My children knew Donovan's son, and told a story about the swimming pool behind his house. Artie, who called his autobiography *Fatso*, was huge in his playing days and got huger afterward. Once, in the winter, when the pool was empty, he fell in after a few drinks too many and no one could pull him out. Legend later grew that a crane had to be brought over to hoist him up.

One time, in the seventies, I went into Artie's liquor store to interview him about the Colts team. I was wearing a slipover shirt that looked vaguely like part of a sailor suit—I had grabbed it in Rome after the airline lost my luggage. Since my wife was not with me at the time, my taste had not been impeccable. Artie, who never disguised his feelings, gave me a queer look and said, "What are you—an Englishman?" He loved to talk about his teammates, including the "weirdo" Berry and the super-human Unitas. He said that Unitas was so accurate with a foot-ball that once, when a defensive player sacked him and rubbed his head in the dirt, he told the apologetic lineman who had let the charger in to let him through again on the next play. As the opposing lineman thundered at him, Unitas jammed the foot-ball around his face mask and broke his nose. It was counted an incomplete pass.

There were many myths about the combination of Unitas throwing and Berry receiving. Berry was so surehanded that in his entire career he had only one fumble. At The Golden Arm, I asked Unitas if he had some special affinity with Berry as a re-ceiver. He said, "Hell no. Raymond bugged me. He wanted to tell me all these fancy steps he would take, the new patterns he was inventing. I told him I did not want to hear that stuff. Just get clear, I told him, and I'll find you." I went to see Berry in Massachusetts, where he had gone after retiring as a player. He was working for the New England Patriots, first as a receivers coach and then as head coach (in his second season at the top spot, he took the team to the Super Bowl).

I repeated to Berry the common myth that he and Unitas shared a single brain, or some invisible connection. His wife, Sally, laughed out loud at the thought. Though the two men had practiced together in the off hours at first, they soon got on each other's nerves. Berry was especially concerned at the stories Unitas would tell about him—stories that entered accounts still being published. Unitas thought he was paying tribute to Berry as a man with little natural talent who overcame all obstacles by hard work and study. In my conversation with him at The Golden Arm, Unitas told me that Berry had one leg shorter than the other. He was also a slow runner, had bad eyes, a bad back, and only nine usable fingers.

Berry especially resented the way Unitas kept telling the story of his short leg after Berry had corrected him. Unitas had once seen the team doctor treating Berry for a pinched nerve in his back. The doctor kept lowering the legs alternately, to see what effect the pinched nerve had on his freedom of motion—which was why Unitas said he had a bad back. Actually, this was a temporary injury that had nothing to do with the permanent state of either Berry's back or his legs. "I used to get letters from parents saying they had a child with one leg shorter than the other, and they knew I was playing football in that condition. I had to convince them that the story was false."

What about the unusable finger? "I use it all the time." His little finger was dislocated and ended up skewed. But he kneaded putty to bring back its strength and flexibility. And his bad eyes? Berry was one of the first athletes to use contact lenses, and he did not have just one set of them. He had a case with a range of options. He had tinted ones when he was running away from the sun—in effect, built-in sunglasses. He had different tints for playing at night under lights. He had experimented for all different conditions. As a result, he had better eyesight than anyone on the field—he could hardly have caught hundreds of passes and dropped only one if that had not been the case. Unitas saw him shifting his contacts about in their special case and thought he must be practically blind.

As for not having natural talent, Berry said that he had very large hands for catching and very large feet (size 14) for cutting, twisting, and reversing. It is true that he studied every aspect of the game with an intensity that a natural athlete like Unitas considered obsessive. But that paid off for him. Berry would go out and pace the field before games, identifying areas of loose turf, slippery wetness, or (in winter) icy or frozen patches. As he had contact lenses for different conditions, he had a range of cleats he could use for the different turfs he had to run on. He could change them in the game as rain or freezing temperatures altered the situation.

Despite their temperamental differences, Berry could not have held Unitas in higher esteem as a player. I told him that many people thought the game had gone beyond the days when Unitas called signals without feedback from specialized experts on their headphones. Berry, who had observed the changes in the game as he coached the New England Patriots, said that he had never seen a better reader of the situation on the field than Unitas. Whatever new things had come in, he told me, all Unitas needed was minimal protection from his linemen and he would find a way to win, against any challenge. "He was just a winner."

Frank Deford, the great writer for *Sports Illustrated*, agreed. As someone who had covered all sports for many years, he had been given many autographs and souvenirs. But he kept only two—a signed basketball from Bill Russell and a signed football from Unitas. He described Unitas as not only the greatest football player he had ever seen but the greatest athlete. When Unitas died in 2002, Deford wrote that whatever other developments had occurred in the game since his retirement, and whoever had played brilliantly at quarterback after him, nonetheless: "If there were one game scheduled, Earth versus the Klingons, with the fate of the universe on the line, any person with his wits about him would have Johnny U. calling signals in the huddle." All of us Baltimorons (as Mencken called us) emphatically agreed.

Shrivers

Another Maryland family I had dealings with in Baltimore was the Shrivers. One day Sargent Shriver came to my house in Baltimore to go over a speech on Jefferson that I wrote for him to give in France. He had earlier asked me to write campaign speeches when he ran for vice president. I told him I do not write politicians' speeches, but he invited me for lunch, and then for dinner, at his home in suburban Maryland. Shriver, who was born in Westminster, Maryland, comes from an old Maryland family. Most people now associate him with the Kennedy family, but his own clan was deeper in history than the Kennedys— his ancestor David Shriver signed the Maryland constitution in 1776. Sarge got rather absorbed by the Kennedys, but he was a striking figure on his own. I once asked the longtime business manager of the *Yale Daily News*, Francis Donahue, who had been the best chairman (chief student editor) of the *News*, and he answered with no hesitation, "Bill Buckley." Second best? Equally unhesitant: "Sarge Shriver."

Shriver's wife, Eunice, was very gracious to me at their home. Their children, Maria and Bobby, came in from playing tennis. Maria, who still had her teenage glow, was radiant. Bobby, who would arrange, as a Yale student, for me to teach a visiting course there, was friendly then and after, when I visited him in California. It was a little different with Eunice. I had met her at a Special Olympics event in Baltimore and wrote a column praising her work. She was grateful then, but she did not stay friendly. She was on the board of directors of Holy Cross College, and she voted with the rest of the board to give me an honorary degree in 1982. But between that vote and the college's commencement, my book *The Kennedy Imprisonment* came out, highly critical of Joseph Kennedy's regimen for his family.

Eunice called the Holy Cross president, Jesuit father Jack Brooks, and said my award had to be rescinded. He told me about that, and how he protested to her that he had no power to cancel the award—the board had voted on it. She said she would get the board to reverse itself. She tried. But at the commencement, after my degree was given me, another member of the board, lawyer Edward Bennett Williams, came up to me, and said, "Did you notice that there was only one board member who was not here?" I said I had not expected her to be there. I know when I'm on another enemies list.

6

Movies

———◆◆✕◆◆———

John Waters, though considered an "underground filmmaker," was a professional in his tastes, as I found when the two of us served on a jury for the Baltimore Film Festival. The jury was made up of four people—a mistake, since even numbers make it hard or impossible to break a tie. The two non-Baltimore judges came from the American Film Institute in neighboring Washington. Waters and I argued that first place should go to a film based on Flannery O'Connor's story "The River." As fellow Catholics, we had a soft spot for O'Connor, and John's affection was strengthened by her gothic weirdness. My son, who has been a part-time filmmaker and was a nonvoting participant in the festival, agreed with John and me. But the AFI people dismissed our film as "too professional." They saw film festivals as meant to encourage the amateur, the experimental, or the "nonslick"—they thought Waters was deserting his own cause when he went with a conventionally filmed religion-themed movie. Long argument failed to budge either side, so the award money was split between two choices, and no first-place prize was given.

I reported on other film festivals, Sundance for *Harper's*, the annual Pordenone (Italy) Silent Film Fest for the *New York Re-*

view, and I taught film in the American Studies Program at Northwestern University. While writing my book on Ronald Reagan, I watched Reagan rarities (like the Brass Bancroft series) on a Moviola in the Republic archives at Madison, Wisconsin. In Los Angeles, I listened to tapes of the Screen Actors Guild meetings at the time of Reagan's prominence in the SAG—I had to go into a closet off the current SAG president's office, since its building was being vacated for a new structure. There were no earphones for the recording machine and I had to keep the volume low, so as not to disturb the president on the other side of the door. On the other hand, I could hear clearly the curses and vulgarities that the president (Patty Duke) shouted over the phone or at someone in her office.

Once a person writes several books about presidents of the United States, editors or agents ask that person to write about each president who comes along. I was asked, then, to write books about Presidents Ford, Carter, Bush I, Clinton, and Bush II. I told those asking that I preferred to write about presidents who were lightning rods, reaction to whom revealed something about the American people. That is what first drew me to the book an editor at Houghton Mifflin wanted about Nixon, or to the all-American Reagan. When I turned down ideas for other presidents, my editor at Simon & Schuster, Alice Mayhew, asked me if there was another figure of that sort who had *not* been a president.

I told her John Wayne was such an outsize figure—a political symbol as well as a film monument, for some the very epitome of patriotism and manliness. His movies had been used as recruiting tools for the marines. Yet John Ford had mocked his favored actor for the way he dodged military service during World War II. Liberals were so offended by his political stands that they foolishly belittled his acting achievements. Since Ford was my favorite American film director after Orson Welles, I welcomed the opportunity to spend many hours with the people who had worked with him and with Wayne. I haunted the film archives at New York's Museum of Modern Art and the Library of Congress, whose curators (Charles Silver and Madeline Matz, respectively) became friends. I read the Ford Papers at the Lilly Library in Indiana, and went to see Andrew McLaglen on his island off the coast of Washington State.

Oliver Stone

But I had never seen a film being made until Oliver Stone's publicist called and asked me to come talk with him about his new project, *Nixon*. I hesitated, because I thought Stone's *JFK* was a laughable distortion of history. He had turned a flamboyant liar, "Big Jim" Garrison of New Orleans, into a quietly wise Atticus Finch, with a porch scene where he rocks his daughter taken straight from *To Kill a Mockingbird*. There were rumors that Stone was going to push his conspiracy theories onto Richard Nixon. But the publicist assured me that, while this was true of the first draft of a script, people who had read it, like Robert Scheer, persuaded him against the idea. These people included Anthony Hopkins, who was playing Nixon in the film. He had at first refused when offered the role—he thought it improper for a Welshman to participate in an attack on an American president.

But Stone told him the characterization of Nixon would be sympathetic—pitying but sympathetic—and the publicist confided to me that Stone had given Hopkins my *Nixon Agonistes*, indicating the approach he would take. So I went to Los Angeles.

The filming was in progress when I arrived. I talked at length to Hopkins. Though he is a wonderful mimic, treating me to takeoffs on Laurence Olivier and John Gielgud, he said he was not going to do a Nixon impression, but would try to get inside the man. He had interviewed his daughters. He had ruled against the effort of makeup people to give him a false nose. Though he did suggest Nixon's hunched-over walk, as a way of getting his spirit, he did not imitate his voice. The result is that this movie draws on *Citizen Kane,* not *To Kill a Mockingbird.* It is the picture of an emotionally wounded man who rises to power without ever becoming a full human being. That was roughly the picture drawn in my book.

Stone had read my Ruby book, because he reads everything about the assassination of Kennedy. He still has a picture of Jim Garrison on his mantel. He wanted to argue about the assassination, but I had learned from experience that discussions with conspiracy theorists are a waste of time. Still, I admired some of his other movies—*Platoon, The Doors, Salvador, Natural Born Killers.* And I was curious about his days studying with Martin Scorsese at NYU. He said, "Marty's love of movies is what he conveyed. In those days, the only place you could see some foreign films in New York was late at night on Channel 11. He would come in the next morning with red eyes and a hungover look from being up all night in front of the TV."

Stone had learned that I was a classicist, and he told me that his fondest dream was to make a movie about Alexander the Great. He had written a script and scouted out locations. Why hadn't he made it? "Not enough money." He wanted an epic scale for this film. I said that Scorsese had made *The Last Temptation of Christ* on a modest budget. "Yeah, and it looks it." When Stone later published his autobiographical novel, I found out what intrigued him in the Alexander story. Stone's French mother, who was separated from his father, tried to seduce him (according to the novel), just as Alexander's mother seduced him. This idea so enthralled Stone that, when he did make *Alexander,* he ridiculously cast Angelina Jolie as Olympias and Colin Farrell as the king, though Farrell is only one year younger than his supposed mother in the movie.

I had heard that Stone bullied his actors. That may have been true in his earlier days, when he was still uncertain of his authority and was using drugs. But he was a model of patience and understanding in the scenes I saw him shoot, and the actors I talked with on the set showed great admiration for him—not only Hopkins but Paul Sorvino (playing Henry Kissinger), James Woods (as H. R. Haldeman), J. T. Walsh (John Ehrlichman), and others. When Stone wanted to instruct an actor, he would take him or her aside rather than correct the person before others. And he took suggestions graciously.

When Joan Allen, playing Pat Nixon, was seated in the front cabin of the Air Force One mockup, she had to listen to Haldeman and Ehrlichman making anti-Semitic comments against the absent Kissinger. She told Stone she felt uncomfortable just sitting there and listening to such talk. Could she do something to signal her lack of ease? Stone said that was a good idea, but what could she do? She suggested that she take a magazine out of the rack in the plane and pointedly start leafing through it. Stone approved the idea, and reshot the scene that way. It did not make it into the commercial cut, though one never knows what factors go into the editing of scenes.

Paul Schrader

I reviewed Martin Scorsese's film *The Last Temptation of Christ* for the *New York Review of Books*. It fascinated me—I still think it the best movie about Jesus—and I called up its writer, Paul Schrader, to discuss it. The film is formed at the confluence of three religious traditions, the Greek Orthodoxy of Nikos Kazantzakis, who wrote the novel on which it is based; the evangelical Protestantism of Schrader; and the Italian Catholicism of Scorsese. The film was widely condemned by religious people. Patrick Buchanan denounced it without ever having seen it. What upset them is that Jesus is seen in bed with Mary Magdalene. But that is a fantasy which Jesus rejects. His "last temptation" is to give up his divine mission and become an ordinary human being, avoiding crucifixion, and having children in a happy home. Instead, he returns to the cross.

As I got to know Schrader better, he told me of his Calvinist upbringing, being forbidden to see movies. His father rejected him when *Last Temptation* came out, even demonstrating against the movie when it ran in a nearby theater. Schrader's alma mater, Calvin College, denounced it (though some students sneaked away to see it in Detroit). Only after many years did the college honor its alumnus with a festival of his films. Schrader invited me to interview him onstage during the festival. His hometown, Grand Rapids, Michigan, had forgiven him for an earlier offense, when he made it the locale of the first film he directed as well as wrote, *Hardcore* (1979). He used the site and its citizens for a scathing picture of Calvinist religiosity and hypocrisy. He said he had to use the town, since he had so little money for this, his first directing job.

I asked, then, how he could afford to hire George C. Scott for the role of the religious father who seeks his straying daughter. Scott had been a big star after he played General Patton in 1970. Schrader explained that Scott was in one of his heavy drinking phases, increasingly hard to insure. Schrader was warned that if he let him get started on a bottle, he would probably not finish the picture. Late one afternoon, there was just one scene that had to be finished before they moved to a new location. Setting the lights was taking a long time, so Scott went to his trailer. When at last the set was ready, Schrader sent for Scott, but the messenger returned and said he would not come. Fearing the worst, Schrader went to the trailer and found Scott with a half-emptied bottle. The director pleaded with him to come out for just one quick scene, the last chance to get the segment finished.

Scott was surly. "I should never have agreed to do this picture. It is a shitty picture, and you are a shitty director." Schrader humored him, and kept pleading. At last Scott said he would go back out on one condition only—that Schrader promise never to direct another picture, for the good of the movie industry.

Schrader solemnly promised, to get the thing done. Years later, Scott spotted Schrader in a Los Angeles restaurant, stomped over, slapped down a *Variety* with news of Schrader's new picture, and said, "You promised never to direct again." Schrader was astonished that he remembered out of his alcoholic mist. He said: "What can I say, George? I lied."

Schrader asked me to do another interview-on-stage event in the East, but I had a different engagement at the time. Then he invited me to see him film a movie in Toronto. The two of us had dinner at an Italian restaurant on the night of my arrival in Canada. One of the first things he asked was, "Do you still go to church?" I answered, "Yes. Do you?" "Yes, but my father would not count it as really going to church. We attend Episcopalian services." Then he told me about the film he was making, *Forever Mine*. It was an old script he had sold years ago. Since the studio did not use it, he bought it back—resenting the interest he had to pay for the intervening years. In the story, a gangster (Ray Liotta) marries a young woman (Gretchen Mol), takes her to Miami, and then neglects her as he gambles. She meets a young beachcomber (Joseph Fiennes) and spends the night in his cabin. When Liotta finds out about this, he has his gang beat and mutilate Fiennes. Sixteen years later, Fiennes, who has had cosmetic surgery and become a gangster himself, goes back to get revenge. Schrader said he was having trouble with Fiennes, who had contracted for this movie before the release of his 1998 hit, *Shakespeare in Love*. He had arrived on the new set with a badly swollen ego, was demanding changes in the script, and generally acting like a spoiled brat.

I asked Schrader about his relations with Martin Scorsese.

After great success as a director-writer team (*Taxi Driver, Raging Bull, The Last Temptation of Christ*), they had a noisy breakup. Schrader said that Scorsese had insisted he be listed as co-scenarist and have the right to change Schrader's scripts. Friends had tried to bring them back together, and after a time they had a tense lunch meeting at which Scorsese promised not to make a single change if Schrader would do a script from the real-life story *Bringing Out the Dead*. Schrader agreed, and Scorsese was making the film in New York even as Schrader made his movie in Canada. I asked if Scorsese was keeping to his agreement. Schrader said he knew that he was because his (Schrader's) wife, Mary Beth Hurt, was acting as the nurse in *Bringing Out*, and she assured him that the script was being observed exactly.

A handsome young man had been eavesdropping on our conversation in the restaurant, and after his dinner he came over, gave Schrader his card, and said he was an actor and would like to audition for Schrader. After he left, Schrader flipped me the card and said, "Look at its credits. He is not an actor. He's a model."

The next day, on the set, I saw what Schrader meant about Fiennes. He was being fitted with a wig and he objected to all the models being given him. The dramatic time of his meeting with Mol was the early 1970s, when men wore their hair long. He did not want that. Schrader kept explaining that his look had to be different from the time of his reappearance in the late 1980s. What did he want? He wanted to wear his own short hair in both eras. The discussion was going nowhere. Schrader came over and whispered that Fiennes might be showing off with a writer on the set, could I step outside for a while?

I went out and talked with one of my heroes, John Bailey, the great director of photography for Schrader's masterpiece, *Mishima*, which is full of dazzling camera effects in both color and black-and-white. Before he did Mishima, he did Schrader's *American Gigolo* and *Cat People*, so he knew the man's habits well and enjoyed working with him. I asked Bailey about a film released at the same time as *Mishima*, Laurence Kasdan's *Silverado*, another tour de force of Bailey's lighting. Bailey would go on to make many fine movies (like *As Good As It Gets*). We shared enthusiasms for directors, past and present, cooling our heels while Fiennes threw his tantrum. After almost half an hour, Schrader came out, and we asked if he had made any progress with the temperamental star. He shook his head dejectedly.

When I met with Schrader a year later, I asked if Fiennes had ever become cooperative. He said he had not, and the morale of the whole team suffered because of it. The movie never did take off. Though it was shown in Spanish and Japanese theaters, no distributor was found for an American release. It went straight to television. Schrader's other film of 1998, *Bringing Out the Dead*, did run in theaters, but it was not a success. I asked Schrader why. "It should have been a gritty little picture, like *Mean Streets*. But Marty cannot do anything small anymore. He has a big entourage he must support, and he needs big stars. The hero of this movie is an emergency ambulance attendant who burns out young because of all the horrors he witnesses. Marty cast Nick Cage in the role, who was too old. He used the wrong music—music from our *Taxi Driver* days. The whole tone was wrong." I asked whatever happened to Joe Fiennes. He shrugged,

"Not much." It has been mainly downhill for him since the brief glory of *Shakespeare in Love*.

Dick Cusack

When I moved to Evanston in 1980, my principal contact with the movies was through Dick Cusack. Though his children are the actors best known to the public, Dick appeared in nineteen movies himself, wrote one of them (*Jack Bull*), and wrote and acted in plays for the Piven Theatre Workshop, the Evanston institution where all the Cusack children trained as actors— Johnny, Joanie, Annie, Susie, and Billy (to give them their Evanston family names). Since Dick often played judges in the movies, he was a natural for the part of Pontius Pilate in our church's annual Lenten enactment of the Passion of Christ. I was always amused by the fact that the director of this event got all her other actors to memorize their parts, but Dick—the only professional in the group—refused to do that. He just read it straight from the Bible.

One of the movies where Dick played a judge was *Eight Men Out*, with his son John and Chicagoan Studs Terkel in the cast, which led to a three-way friendship. I brought Studs and Joan Cusack to my American Studies class to talk about movie-making. (I would have brought Dick, but he had died by then.) The Cusack home was on a park beside Lake Michigan, and every Thanksgiving during Dick's lifetime the family and friends played a game of touch football in the park. Dick, who was on the championship basketball team at Holy Cross with Bob

Cousy, had back troubles that kept him from playing, but he served as referee, making up creative penalties, such as "Five yards for calling a stupid play." Dick's wit never deserted him. When he was dying of cancer, and his son John asked if there was someone he wanted to see before he died, he answered, "Yeah. Ava Gardner." John and Joan both left the movies they were making to spend their father's last months with him. John took him to the Mayo Clinic and other places to see if there was any way the cancer could be arrested. John told me that when one medication caused diarrhea, Dick came out of the bathroom saying, "That was the most massive evacuation since Dunkirk." At Dick's funeral, after the service in our campus church, the pianist was called up, and John said to the congregation, "Don't think we're being irreverent. This is what Dad asked to be played." The pianist launched into "Ain't Misbehavin'" by Fats Waller.

7

Voices

———◆◆×◆◆●———

W hen I met Natalie, my wife-to-be, one of the first things
we learned about each other was that we love opera. We
did not agree on everything. Among tenors, I preferred Beniamino Gigli while she liked Giuseppe di Stefano. I later learned
that Luciano Pavarotti and his tenor father had the same split,
the father staying with Gigli while his son defected to di Stefano. Most of the time, though, Natalie's and my tastes were in
accord. When we were dating, we could go in from New Haven
to New York on Saturdays and line up for standing-room tickets
at the Old Met, both matinee and evening performances. After
the afternoon show, I would take up a position in the night line
while she bought sandwiches and brought them for us to eat as
we waited. After the evening performance, we took a late train
back to New Haven.

Standing in those lines was a real education, since the devo-
tees were old-time aficionados. They had institutional memories of the place, and encyclopedic recollections of their favorite
singers' past performances. I experienced that fanatical devo-
tion to singers that James McCourt has so compellingly depicted
in his novels. Standing in line reminded me of the music students who jostle for a place in the cheap gallery ("the gods") of

the movie *The Red Shoes.* When I got back to Yale, I would compare notes with a fan of Anna Moffo—he had followed her on tour, but was now forced to sell his records to stay in graduate school.

A friend of mine is writing a book about his early attraction to music—all about the complex interplay of parts, the meeting of mathematics and sensuous pleasure, acoustical structure, and all that. My interest was from the outset more simple and visceral. I loved the many uses of the human voice. Even in high school, four recorded voices especially thrilled me—those of Judith Anderson, John Barrymore, Fyodor Chaliapin (as it was spelled then), and Jose Ferrer. I heard records of Judith Anderson performing Robinson Jeffers's *Medea* and her Lady Macbeth with Maurice Evans. As Medea, she baritoned the lines

Men boast their battles. I tell you this, and we know it.
It is easier to stand in battle *three* times, in the *front line,*
IN THE STABBING FURY, than to bear one child.

As Lady Macbeth, she answered her husband's fear of failing: "*We? Fail?* But screw-your-courage-to-the-sticking-place, and WE'LL / NOT / FAIL!" Hers was the best woman actor's voice I knew till I heard Pamela Brown do *The Lady's Not for Burning* or Glenda Jackson as Chorus in *Murder in the Cathedral.*

John Barrymore recorded only one soliloquy from *Hamlet* and one from *Richard III* during his brief Shakespearean time (1920–25) before the booze got to his voice and memory. He quickens his rhythm magically at "I'll *have* these players *play*-something-like-the-murder-of-my-*father* before mine *uncle.* [Rising voice] I'll observe his *looks*. I'll *tent* him to the *quick*. If he do BLENCH, [Falling voice] I / KNOW / MY / COURSE."

I heard Chaliapin sing the death of Boris Godunov in one of the old music stores of the 1940s that had listening booths. I could not afford to buy the record, but I went back several times to hear it over. I did not know what the words meant, but listening to the man's beautiful barking was like hearing a cave sing. That was the beginning of my love for opera. I heard Chaliapin on a 33⅓ rpm LP (long play as they were known then), but when I went to the Carnegie Library in my hometown (Adrian, Michigan), they still had 78 rpm shellac discs for loaning out. I toted them home. When I took out the multidisc recording of Mozart's *Magic Flute* (in two albums) it was too bulky for me to manage on my bicycle, so I had to walk all the way home with it weighing on my arms, and then go back for my bike.

When I visited a friend's home, we listened to old 78 rpm records of *Othello*. Most people remark the voice of Paul Robeson in the title role. I was more interested in Ferrer's performance as Iago, the way he could softly stab Othello with words: Did Cassio lie with Desdemona? "With her, *on her*, what you will." Shortly after I had heard this tour de force of sly malice, I heard Ferrer twirl out sweet phrases under the balcony as Cyrano de Bergerac in the 1950 movie. I met Ferrer in 1957. The conservative newspaperman Willard Edwards introduced us. Conservatives admired him then because liberals detested him, after he made friendly noises to the anti-Communists in Hollywood. But I realized it was not his politics that prevented him from becoming a big movie star. Short men have a hard time getting to the top in that world. The only other short movie actor I met,

85

Paul Newman—I talked with him during Eugene McCarthy's presidential race—succeeded because he was spectacularly good-looking, which Ferrer, for all his great voice, was not.

The most impressive voices, of course, belong to opera singers. The opera voice is a freak of nature. It surpasses others in size, range, flexibility, and speed. It can trill, spin dazzling fioriture, dive far down and soar far up. The first time I was able to experience a classically trained voice close up was also in high school. There was a marvelous program, back in the 1940s, called Community Concerts. Great artists were sent around to remote communities and schools. I heard the Trapp Family (long before *The Sound of Music*) and the Russian Cossack Singers (in the original cultural exchange program), but mainly I was impressed by Todd Duncan, the classical music professor from Howard University who was George Gershwin's original Porgy in *Porgy and Bess*.

At my high school, Duncan sang Schubert songs and Mussorgsky's "Song of the Flea." But he ended with excerpts from *Porgy*. It was all moving musicianship, and though I never heard him again live, I retained an interest in his records and his life. Like other black artists of the time, he was unable to register in hotels of the cities where he sang and had to be put up in private homes. I read later how Gershwin had found him while searching for a black baritone of operatic quality. Duncan was recommended as a professor of music, and he showed up at Gershwin's Manhattan apartment carrying his classical songs. Duncan had never heard Gershwin's music. He was a classical music scholar who looked down on popular songs. Asked to sit down at one of the grand pianos in the Gershwin apartment, he sang a piece he had brought with him. When he finished, Gershwin asked him to stand in the elbow of the piano so he could see what he looked like while he sang out, not looking down at the piano. Duncan said he would have to take the music sheet with him, and Gershwin said that was all right—he would play it while Duncan sang. Gershwin needed to hear music only once to repeat it at the keyboard. Duncan said, "That is when I knew I was dealing with a real musician."

I met another great singer of the Porgy role, William Warfield, at my own university, Northwestern, where he taught music while I was in the history department. The former husband of Leontyne Price, Warfield was in his seventies when I knew him, but he was still singing beautifully, though in diminished range and volume. He sat at the piano to sing selections from the *Old American Songs* of Aaron Copland that he had premiered, and told us about working over them with the composer. When I heard Thomas Hampson sing them in the White House, I was able to tell him a story that Warfield had passed on. In the song "I Bought Me a Cat," where the singer imitates the sounds various animals make, Copland had written that the cow says "Unh! Unh!" imitating the actual bellow of a cow. But Warfield complained that everyone wants the cow to say, "Moo! Moo!" So Copland made the change. Hampson, who adored Warfield, was glad to hear this bit of musical history.

I never realized the sheer size of the opera voice till I stood onstage next to Beverly Sills as she was rehearsing for a recital with her pianist. She was thought of as having a rather small voice by the standards of her peers (like Joan Sutherland). But my ears were ringing as she sang so near me, and I wondered how singers saved their own eardrums when they were loosing voices of this power directly into each other's faces.

Sills was rehearsing a Rachmaninoff song, and she had taken coaching for its pronunciation from her mother, an emigrant from Odessa. (The mother had fled an anti-Jewish pogrom in an empty pickle barrel and come into America through Canada.) I came to know "Mama Sills," as she was called, over the years. At her house for a birthday party, her Russian language skills were at issue, since she could not understand the Yiddish dirty jokes Danny Kaye was telling. She asked what he was saying, and the conductor Julius Rudel told her, "You don't want to know."

Mama Sills's real name was Shirley Silverman. She was a warm and generous person, widely loved in the circle of her famous daughter. I first met her when I was writing an article on Beverly. After she had told me about her daughter, she typically said, "I am very proud of Beverly. But I am just as proud of my sons, so let me tell you about them"—her two sons, a doctor and a publisher. When she had described them in detail, she asked me to tell her about my children. Her interest was genuine. She said, "Do you praise them enough?" I said, "I hope so." "You must. If they do nothing more spectacular than tying their shoe, you must make them see that as a great achievement." Mama Sills asked to hear from my children, and they corresponded with her. When my daughter went to New York to work as a literary agent, Mama Sills took her to lunch and invited her to her home. When my son, who was a fan of musical theater, visited New York, Mama took him backstage to converse with Yul Brynner after a performance of *The King and I*.

Mama's was the wisdom that kept Beverly grounded in a life of great suffering—she had a mentally troubled son, a deaf daughter with multiple sclerosis, a stepdaughter with legal troubles, and (eventually) a husband with Alzheimer's disease. Though Beverly was nicknamed "Bubbles" for her bouncy attitude, she was a fiercely determined professional, as Julius Rudel found when he opened a new house for the New York City Opera at Lincoln Center. Beverly had been his most durable star in the old house, and she felt he owed it to her to open the new theater. Rudel was putting on Handel's *Giulio Cesare,* and he had slated Phyllis Curtin for the splashy coloratura role of Cleopatra. Sills told him that if he did that, she would leave Rudel's company and have "Pete" (Peter Greenough, her wealthy husband) rent Carnegie Hall, where she would sing all the Cleopatra arias in a way that would make Rudel's production look sickly. She won, and it was her performance as Cleopatra that lifted her from fame to superstardom for the rest of her career.

She was usually cunning enough that she did not have to resort to threats. When she made her debut at La Scala in Milan, the opera director tried to achieve exotic effects in Rossini's *Siege of Corinth* by the use of scrims over the stage. Singers do not like the psychological effect of an obstacle between their voices and the audience, so they protested. But the director was unbending. That is when, Beverly told me, she informed the conductor that she would have trouble following his baton if she had to peer through a scrim. Instantly the scrims came down. She was good at getting her way, using skills that she deployed on singers, directors, conductors, and donors when, after she stopped singing, she became the manager of the New York City Opera and chairwoman of the board of both Lincoln Center and the Metropolitan Opera. She was always smart and clear in what she did, beginning as a mathematical whiz in school. Her piano coach, Roland Gagnon, told me, "She sight-reads music like lightning, and can memorize a score in no time, even on an airplane." When I sat with her in her dressing room before *Lucia* or *Anna Bolena*, she sometimes worked a double crostic while we chatted. Despite her sunny smile, she had a formidable intellect. When I asked her why she never sang in *Rigoletto*, which seemed made for her voice, she shrugged. "Gilda is such a dope." She did not find it fun pretending to be dumb.

Becoming the boss at the Met was an ironic triumph for Beverly, since the autocratic Met manager Rudolf Bing had insulted her in her early career and vowed she would never sing in his house. When he retired and she made her belated Met debut, she was given an eighteen-minute ovation at the end of her first performance there. But in a manner typical of her (and of her mother), she visited Bing when he was hospitalized late in life. Her charitable activities were as extensive as her managerial ones.

The many sides of Beverly came out in her letters to me, of which I'll quote just one:

Dear Garry,

You've been on my mind these last few weeks—so much so that I smiled when your book came, and though I was delighted to hear from you I wasn't in the least bit surprised. The book goes with me to Martha's Vineyard June 22nd, so you'll undoubtedly be hearing from me again, and thank you for sending it.

It's been an horrendous year for us. Exactly a year ago, following open heart surgery, Pete had a stroke—he was severely impaired—miraculously he's 90 percent back, totally self-sufficient, mobile and with only a trace of aphasia. I'm so grateful.

Muffy's M.S. is constantly on the attack—chronic and non-remitting but she goes to her office every day and fights the battle. My daughter is an awesome human being.

I am holding together and still shaking my fist at God. I miss Mom terribly. What a void. Write me some more! Call me if you get to NY. Please. Love and hugs, Bev

Things got tougher and tougher for Beverly. Peter's Alzheimer's progressed to the point where he no longer recognized her, but she went every day to visit him in his care center, despite her Lincoln Center duties. Muffy had to move about in a wheelchair and could not leave her mother's apartment building.

As her troubles mounted, she asked me to lunch with her whenever I was in New York. Across from Lincoln Center, we would meet at Fiorello, where there was a booth named for her. Because she knew I loved her mother (back when old ladies mothered me), she began to confide her problems, which she did not want to air in her professional role as board chairperson. She had to find a new apartment with a pool where Muffy could swim. She marveled at Peter's serenity, derived from medication. "Pete's so nice now. He was never *nice*." Greenough had a caustic wit, which he sometimes used on Beverly's groupies. He once asked if I was a freelance writer. I said no, I taught at a university. He laughed: "Good. 'Freelance writer' is just a polite name for 'unemployed.'" When Peter read in the paper that I had turned down an award from the Sons of the American Revolution because the speaker before the presentation of the award had been applauded for a right-wing diatribe, Peter wrote me a letter of congratulation, saying that he had turned down membership in that group several years earlier when they endorsed conservative positions. It bothered Peter that Beverly sang in Nixon's White House, but she convinced him that her duty to promote opera overrode her own revulsion at the Vietnam War.

At our lunches, Beverly worried about attendance and donations slacking off at the Met. She was hatching some of the tactics that her successor, Peter Gelb, would use to make opera more accessible. Like her mother, she always wanted to know about my children. She never pined for her singing days. She had determined beforehand to retire at age fifty, and not to hang on to followers while her powers declined, as so many singers do—Callas, Tebaldi, and Sutherland among them. Beverly admired Rosa Ponselle, who had retired at the height of her career. Beverly had sung briefly for Rosa's Baltimore opera company. After my wife and I moved to Baltimore, we occasionally saw Rosa around town, and visited her Villa Pace home in the countryside. When Rosa visited Johns Hopkins, she brought with her the screen test made of her *Carmen* performance, using the best sound equipment of the time. From the back of the room she shouted that the volume should be turned up: "Louder! I had a *big* voice." When Licia Albanese visited Rosa, I got to talk with the first Mimì I had heard at the Met. I asked her about the earliest opera she ever recorded, when she was Mimì to Beniamino Gigli's Rodolfo. I wanted to hear about his voice, but she just remembered his thoughtfulness to a young soprano: "He brought me sandwiches when I was feeling tired."

Ponselle was a personal hero to my wife Natalie's Italian community in Connecticut. Rosa had been born in the same Meriden hospital where Natalie and many of her relatives (and my son) were born. Rosa and her sister Carmela had sung on the Keith Vaudeville Circuit as the teenage "Ponzillo Sisters" before Enrico Caruso heard Rosa and brought her to the attention of the Met manager of the time. She made her debut in the opera that opened the 1918 season, *La Forza del Destino*, when she was only twenty-two. Caruso was from Naples, like Rosa's parents, and he called her Scugnizza (street urchin) in their native dialect. As she stood in the wings for her first entry onto an opera stage, he went over to her and said, "I always get nervous at an opening. Would you please hold my hand?" Great singers are sometimes simply great. Of Rosa's first night, the *New York Times* wrote that the Met had discovered "vocal gold." The soprano Geraldine Farrar famously said that, when comparing singers, you must first place two outside the contest, Caruso and Ponselle, then you could begin ranking the rest.

Another singer I got to know well in several cities was Shirley Verrett, who had overcome the same kind of racist problems that Todd Duncan faced. Leopold Stokowski tried to book her for his Houston Symphony Orchestra in the 1950s, but Texas racists on his board blocked the move. Only when he returned to Philadelphia could he perform and record with her. Her sensitivity to racial issues made her reject the role of Bess in *Porgy*—

she felt the stereotypes were too condescending. Her independent judgment made her take heretical positions. Though she was a strong and convincing actress, she did not adopt Maria Callas as her ideal, since Callas's top notes were too "screechy"—she told me they made her think of playing a comb through cellophane. Though Verrett began as a mezzo-soprano, her brilliant high coloratura made her just as convincing as a soprano, and some of her greatest roles—like Verdi's Lady Macbeth—were performed in that register.

My interest in voices was not channeled entirely toward opera. In 1959, I heard at Stratford-upon-Avon Charles Laughton, playing Bottom in *A Midsummer Night's Dream*, memorably say, "I will *roar* you as gently as any sucking dove; I will *roar* you an 'twere any nightingale." Two of the greatest voices of the twentieth century belonged to John Gielgud and Laurence Olivier, whom I heard perform both in England and in America. In 1959, Olivier repeated the triumph he had achieved twenty years earlier in *Coriolanus*. It was said that he could not repeat the athleticism of his first run, but he surpassed it. When Aufidius called him "Boy," Olivier ran up an incline and took a dive out from the top, straight at the audience, something he had done in his *Hamlet* movie, imitating John Barrymore's dive in the film *Don Juan*. In order to get insurance in the role in 1959, Olivier had to hire professional acrobat "catchers" to grip him in midair. He so concentrated on impulsive athletics that he almost threw away the play's words. Those are better served by Richard Burton in his dazzling recording of the play. But Olivier could concentrate all his verbal artistry in one word. When the actor playing Aufidius called him a "boy of tears," Olivier answered "BOY?" and it was miraculous how much pride, scorn, contempt, and defiance he could pack into a single syllable.

We had seen Gielgud in London in 1959; but my most vivid memory of him was of his 1976 performance in New York of Harold Pinter's *No Man's Land*. The play is practically a two-man tour de force, in which Gielgud played with his old partner, Ralph Richardson. The latter had resisted the role, saying, "Johnny, I'm too old to memorize all those lines." The two of them supplied what was in effect a chamber-music study of all that human voices can suggest in support of each other. During the break between acts, I stepped out under the marquee, where people were huddling against a light drizzle of rain. In the gutter by the curb, the actor Peter Boyle was pacing back and forth in fierce concentration, paying no attention to the rain. I could not resist asking him, as he turned to go back into the theater, what he thought of the performance. He shook his head in disbelief and said, "They can't do that. Nobody can do that."

That was the best tribute I ever heard to the human voice. It is a continuing wonder to me that, of all the million sounds a human being can make, we still recognize a particular voice on the telephone. Saint Augustine once marveled that God can take the few components of the human face and still make each set of features individual, not mistakable for any other. I feel the same about voices, and when I hear Natalie's on the phone, I melt.

8

Nixon

———◆◆✕◆◆———

I first got involved in presidential politics by accident. In 1967, I had taken my wife and three children to my parents' home in Michigan for the Christmas vacation. I got a phone call from Harold Hayes, the *Esquire* editor, who asked me if I could fly immediately to New Hampshire. Murray Kempton, whom he had asked to cover Nixon's attempted comeback in that state's primary, had canceled for family reasons. I flew out, missing Christmas with my family for the second time at Harold's behest (the first time was when he sent me to Dallas to write about Jack Ruby). This time I fell into a political situation for which I had no experience. I was lucky enough to meet with some friendly journalists who knew more than I did, people like Jim Dickenson, Jack Germond, and Jules Witcover. Jim Dickenson and his wife, Mollie, also a journalist, became and remain especially close friends. One day when Nixon ghosted himself away for unannounced TV tapings, leaving the press crew with nothing to do, Jim and I tried to ski for the first time in our lives. Neither was deft, but I was the prime goof, going backward on the beginners' slope.

To follow the New Hampshire primary, as my earliest exposure to presidential politics, was a blessing, especially in 1967, before twenty-four-hour cable exposure had made the event national, scrutinized by hundreds of commentators. There was still a local and intimate feel to the process. Candidates crisscrossed each other in that tiny cockpit, where teams of reporters mingled and compared notes daily. I saw George Romney's flameout when he said he had supported the Vietnam War because he was "brainwashed" by government guides on his trip there.

When Nixon took a break from the New Hampshire primary to set up the race in Wisconsin, his entourage was still small enough to be fitted, staff and journalists, in a DC-3 with only twenty seats in the economy section. After short hops about Wisconsin, we boarded a plane for a night flight to Chicago, and Pat Buchanan, his press aide, led me up into the darkened first-class section for an interview with Nixon. Under the dim overhead light, it was my first close-up opportunity to observe the famous nose. I suppose these words in my *Esquire* article, more than anything else, earned a place for me on Nixon's later enemies list:

> In pictures, its most striking aspect is the ski-jump silhouette ("Bob Hope and I would make a great ad for Sun Valley") but the aspect that awes one when he meets Nixon is its distressing width, accentuated by the depth of the ravine running down its center, and by its general fuzziness. Nixon's "five o'clock shadow" extends all the way up to his heavy eyebrows, though—like many hairy men—he is balding above the brows' "timber line." The nose swings far out; then, underneath, it does not rejoin

his face in a straight line, but curves back up again, leaving a large but partially screened space between nose and lip. The whole face's lack of jointure is emphasized by the fact that he has no very defined upper lip (I mean the lip itself, the thing makeup men put lipstick on, not the moustache area). The mouth works down solely, like Charlie McCarthy's—a rapid but restricted motion, not disturbing the heavy luggage of jowl on either side. When he smiles, the space under his nose rolls up (not in) like the old sunshades hung on front porches. The parts all seem to be worked by wires.

Despite Pat Buchanan's anger when the *Esquire* article came out in April 1968, some of *Esquire*'s editors thought I was too sympathetic to Nixon. I argued that he was not a right-wing extremist but an intellectually serious and prepared candidate, though one insecure and defensive. I also got in trouble with later friends, from Lillian Hellman to I. F. Stone, by continuing to say what I maintained in the article and the book—that Nixon was right in believing that Alger Hiss was a traitor.

Two things from my first coverage of Nixon's New Hampshire and Wisconsin primaries made me think he was not the cartoon figure of liberal myth. I asked Nixon on the airplane to Chicago what book had most influenced him. That is now a common question given to candidates, but I had never heard of it in 1968, and I continued to use it with dozens of politicians after that. Many answers were expectable, and they told me little. For instance, when Pat Buchanan ran for president himself, I asked him the question and he said that Bill Buckley's *God and*

Man at Yale was the one (the book was a plea to alumni to cut off funds for Yale that actually made them give more). When Gary Bauer was running a silly right-wing campaign for president, he told me that Whittaker Chambers's *Witness* had been the main book for him (the same one William Kristol told Dan Quayle to say that he was studying when he was vice president). But Nixon's answer to me was the most thoughtful and revealing I would ever hear.

Nixon mentioned several books, but the one he stressed most, and we discussed most, was Claude Bowers's biography of Albert Beveridge. This was unexpected on its face—Bowers was a Democratic friend of Franklin Roosevelt, who appointed him ambassador to Spain. And Beveridge was a Republican admirer of Federalists like John Marshall (about whom he wrote a four-volume biography, winner of a Pulitzer Prize). Nixon, in other words, was not giving a party-line symbolic answer, but speaking from his own deep reading. And the answer made sense for Nixon at the time. Beveridge was a Progressive Republican ally of Theodore Roosevelt, Bowers was a Progressive Democrat of the Woodrow Wilson sort, and Nixon had been telling me that he thought a Wilsonian American replacement of the British Empire's worldwide influence was the new mission of America. Neoconservatives would take this idea of spreading democracy by arms to an extreme at the start of the twenty-first century, but Nixon had a milder version of the idea already in the 1960s.

The second thing that made me place Nixon outside the right-wing stereotype was a conversation I had with one of his old friends, ex-congressman from Milwaukee Charles Kersten. I looked up Kersten while we were in Wisconsin, since I knew him from staying at his house when I traveled with his sons, my debate partners in high school. Kersten was a Catholic anti-Communist who knew the activist "labor priest" John Cronin. He told me that Cronin had been Nixon's speechwriter during his vice-presidential days. The priest had met Nixon before then, when Nixon was a senator bringing charges against Alger Hiss. Cronin had intimate ties with the FBI from his efforts to root out Communist influence in the labor unions, and his closest contact in the Bureau was Ed Hummer. Kersten told me that, through Cronin, Hummer fed information on Hiss to Nixon.

I went to interview Father Cronin, and found that his connection with Nixon was even more intimate than Charlie Kersten had told me. Despite the misgivings of his superiors in the Sulpician order, Cronin was allowed to become an unofficial member of Nixon's staff in order to pursue the Catholic Church's opposition to "godless Communism." Cronin told me things I felt were too intimate to put in my initial *Esquire* article or in the book that followed. It was commonly thought and said that Nixon's wife, Pat, was uncomfortable in politics (something I surely observed on the campaign plane) and that she had resisted Nixon's re-entry into politics for the 1968 campaign. After his bruising losses to Kennedy in the 1960 presidential race and to Pat Brown in the 1962 California governor's race, she thought that part of her life was mercifully closed.

I asked Father Cronin if that was his view, too. He said that was definitely true. He had become very friendly with Nixon's whole family—he was especially fond of his daughter Julie. Pat Nixon told Cronin that her husband had promised he would never go back into politics after the California race, which ravaged them both. When he did decide to run in 1968, she found out about it in a newspaper, according to Cronin. But he said that her unhappiness had dated from long before that. Even while Nixon was Eisenhower's vice president, there had been trouble. Cronin discovered this when he went to see Nixon in one of his regular stops at the vice president's office. Nixon told him he needed some papers from his home in suburban Virginia (this was before the vice presidents took over the Naval Observatory in the District), and asked if he would get them for him. But when Cronin knocked on the door of the Nixon home, Pat answered, and said, "Oh no! He can't get back in by sending a priest!"—and she slammed the door. Cronin went back to Nixon and asked, "What did you get me into?" Nixon said, "Oh, I didn't think she would bring it up with you. We have been having some trouble." After this, Cronin observed that Nixon, who had a hotel room in the District for when he presided late at night over the Senate, had stayed at the hotel for weeks.

As I say, I did not write this part of Cronin's story in my *Esquire* article; but I did write about Ed Hummer leaking to Nixon some FBI files on Hiss. Without my knowing it, I had introduced two new names—Cronin and Hummer—into the endlessly heated debates over the Hiss case (a debate I would later go over with Lillian Hellman). People asked why Nixon had to wait for Whittaker Chambers to give him the records he hid in a pumpkin if Nixon was being fed hot items all along from the FBI. Some leftists felt that my report proved Nixon was part of an FBI plot to frame Hiss. Some conservatives thought that what the FBI gave Nixon (if anything) was not conclusive enough for him to act on before Chambers gave him "the Pumpkin Papers." The debate continues, as one can see from the biography written about Father Cronin.[1] The argument centers on Nixon and Hiss, on anti-Communism; but Father Cronin convinced me that his main work for Nixon was on civil rights, and it is true that people were surprised (when they paid attention) by what liberal things Nixon said about blacks. Some have given Daniel Patrick Moynihan the credit for this unexpected side to Nixon's record; but I believe that Father Cronin had more to do with it.

I submitted the *Esquire* article in February 1968, and it came out in April (when the May issue appeared). It was written before the New Hampshire primary (March 8), but I knew it would appear after it. Harold had explained to me his lead-time problem: the high production values and artwork of *Esquire* made publication lag behind the processing of copy. I wrote something I hoped would stand up whether Nixon won or lost New Hampshire, and I thought that was the end of my involvement in presidential elections. But I soon got a phone call from Dorothy de Santillana, an editor at the Houghton Mifflin publishing house in Boston. She had read the article and told me, "You *have* to write a book about Nixon." I replied that I had now said everything I knew about him—and besides, I did not think he could win in November. (So much for my political prescience.) She maintained that what I wrote about America—its conflicted Cold War liberalism—was what she wanted to hear more of, whether Nixon won or lost.

I was not convinced. She said, "Would you at least come up from Baltimore to New York, and let me go down from Boston, to talk this over?" I did not know then what I learned later, that

Dorothy had a gift for getting the first book (or the first important one) from writers she set her sights on—she had edited early books from David Halberstam and Robert Stone. She was married to the Renaissance historian at MIT, Giorgio de Santillana, and she had a wide cultural vision which, at our New York dinner, she fit my article into.

At that dinner, I said that I could not write her book even if I wanted to, since I had just signed a contract with *Esquire* calling for me to write four articles a year, which would not leave me time to follow Nixon's campaign. Dorothy was not easily deterred. She asked if I would consider the book if she persuaded Harold Hayes at *Esquire* to accept several chapters of it as articles under my contract. He did agree with her, and I wrote *Esquire* articles on Nixon's Checkers speech and on his vice-presidential candidate, Spiro Agnew, as parts of the book.

After taking on the book assignment, I boarded Nixon's campaign plane (a far bigger deal than the one he was flying in January, when I had first joined him). By this time, Pat Buchanan, who had not liked my *Esquire* article, tried to discourage people from talking with me—though I beat him to Nixon's brother and many others who had known Nixon in California and elsewhere. Dorothy de Santillana read each draft of the book and found me some extra advances as it grew in bulk. She went to bat for me with other editors when they tried to kill my title, *Nixon Agonistes*—they said no one could pronounce the second word, people would be intimidated by it, afraid to ask for it in bookstores. She pointed out that two of the most famous poems in the English language were Milton's *Samson Agonistes* and Eliot's *Sweeney Agonistes*. When the book came out, she arranged for a launch party at Sardi's in New York, and the senior publishing board came down from Boston for it.

One of the board members, sitting across from me at table, got fuddled with wine and began berating his son at Harvard, saying he was tearing down everything his father believed in. The son was a radical demonstrating against the Vietnam War. His father said, "If I went back tonight and saw him across the barricades, I could shoot him myself." When I met my current literary agent, Andrew Wylie, I told him that story, since the board member was his father and the son he talked about was Andrew.

The hardcover of *Nixon Agonistes* was well enough received, but it positively took off in paperback, after the first Watergate reports began to circulate. I was told during a visit to Yale that it was being taught in four or five different courses there, and I still run across people who say they were introduced to it in college classes. Some say that it inspired them to become journalists, since I made that seem so exciting. I was often told that the book predicted the Watergate scandal—which is not true.

Still, one of the things I noticed on the campaign plane had seeds of future trouble for Nixon. There was a team of stenographers who rotated back to the plane from each campaign stop where Nixon spoke. I asked them what they were up to. It turns out that one man would take down a record of Nixon's speech and go back to type it up, while another man remained at the campaign site to take down Nixon's responses to any questions he was asked. Working at top speed with backup typists, they would have a record of that stop by the time he reached the next one. These records silted up in huge piles at the back of the plane. I asked what was the point. Admittedly, in 1968 there were not cameras and microphones everywhere all the time, as there would be later; but I pointed out that his campaign speech varied little from one place to another, and there would be a record in journalists' tape recorders and notes. But I was told that Nixon did not trust anyone else to be true to what he said, since they were all out to get him. He wanted a record he alone controlled, to challenge any misrepresentations and false extrapolations from his words, and he wanted it from moment to moment. This omnidirectional mistrust would blossom into the break-ins and spying that brought Nixon down. To guard against his enemies, he gave his enemies all their ammunition.

What I said about Hiss and Nixon continued to come up in my life. In 1974 I was teaching a course on the Cold War at Johns Hopkins. Hiss, who had edited the Hopkins student paper in his time at the university, was visiting the campus. A current editor of the paper was taking the course, and he asked if Hiss could visit the class. I said of course. As I have noted, I knew Hiss from the Harrisburg trial of Philip Berrigan. We had conversed there civilly, and I had no reason to think there would be tension in having him address my students.

But just before our class Nixon released a first (heavily edited) collection of the tapes he had made in the Oval Office. I drove to D.C. from Baltimore to get the transcripts from the Government Printing Office, read them quickly through the night, and told Hiss the next morning that he was frequently mentioned in the tapes. He did not know this yet, and I asked if I could read the passages about him to the class and get his comments. He agreed. On the tapes, Nixon repeatedly told staffers how shrewdly he had handled the Hiss investigation, offering that as a model for how to handle the Watergate scandal. Hiss rightly pointed out that there was no parallel between the two episodes. But my students, who had studied his court record, asked Hiss embarrassing questions. I did not pursue those, since I felt I was the host on the occasion. Hiss wrote me a letter afterward, thanking me for my courteous and fair treatment in the class.

Four years after that class I reviewed Allen Weinstein's book on Hiss, *Perjury*, concluding that Hiss had in fact been a traitor, though the statute of limitations left him liable only to perjury charges. Hiss, I was told by a lawyer for the *New York Review of Books*, regularly brought lawsuits against anyone who charged him with treason. Whether he meant to follow through with the action or not, the suits were meant to discourage people from questioning Hiss's loyalty. The lawyer asked me if I had had any dealings with Hiss that would let him claim I was acting from malice. When I produced his letter thanking me for the kind treatment in my classroom, the lawyer said that would be the end of the suit.

Hiss was the occasion for one of my arguments with Lillian Hellman. She not only thought Hiss innocent, but thought Nixon had knowingly framed him. I met Lillian when she held a private conference on the possibility of impeaching President Nixon at Katonah, New York, in 1971. I was invited because *Nixon Agonistes* had appeared the previous year. Raoul Berger's book *Impeachment* was in galleys, and he read parts of it to the gathering. Others invited included the nuclear physicist Philip Morrison, Hannah Arendt, Robert Silvers, and Jules Feiffer. I was asked to be rapporteur, summarizing the discussions at the end of the meeting. Since Lillian liked how I did that, she invited me to write an introduction to her book *Scoundrel Time*.

I accepted, thinking she would send me the text at my home. But no, she said I would have to come to her home on Martha's Vineyard and stay with her while she read her drafts to me. She was very nervous about letting any text get away from her fussy ministrations—the result, I guess, of her trying out play manuscripts with producers and actors. She was known publicly for an aggressive manner, but I had heard from her lawyer Joseph Rauh how nervous she was as they prepared for her appearance before the House Un-American Activities Committee. I found her oddly shy. After we went swimming, she would not take off her swimming cap until I went out of the room—she did not want me to see her hair before she dried and arranged it.

As she read her book to me, I tried to correct one thing. She said the story of Whittaker Chambers hiding the Hiss microfilms in a pumpkin on his farm was ridiculous because they would have rotted in the pumpkin. I said he hid the microfilms only overnight, so they could not be seized by Hiss's agents. But she refused to believe any such story. She was one of those who could never trust Nixon and never doubt Hiss. Even after the Venona intercepts were released in 1995, which should have removed all reasonable doubt about Hiss's guilt, true believers and Nixon haters refused to recognize the obvious.

NOTES

1. John T. Donovan, *Crusader in the Cold War: A Biography of Fr. John F. Croning, S.S. (1908–1994)* (Peter Lang, 2005).

9

Carter and Others

———◆◆◆◆◆———

I got involved with Jimmy Carter's campaign, as with Richard Nixon's, by accident. When Arthur Bremer shot George Wallace during Wallace's second run for the presidency in 1972, Clay Felker, the editor of *New York*, asked me to survey the South to see what effect this would have on the presidential race that year. I started calling politicians and reporters in the southern states, and when I got the office of Jimmy Carter, Georgia's governor, his press secretary, Jody Powell, came on the line and said that the governor would be glad to talk with me if I would just come down to Atlanta. A memo from the time was later published, telling how Powell and Hamilton Jordan had mapped a strategy for getting reporters to raise Carter's national profile for a run at the White House—and my name was on the list of journalists to court.

When I got to Atlanta, Powell said that the governor was about to fly to Tifton in south Georgia to talk with a group of sheriffs who were grumbling against his racial policies. We got on the governor's small plane and he began teasing me about big-shot New Yorkers (he did not know I was from Baltimore, not New York, and had in fact been born in Atlanta). When we got to the sheriffs' meeting, Carter was not intimidated by the clear hostility some of the men displayed when he went into their room. When he rose to speak, he did not preach to them or use liberal talking points. He spoke their language, saying their mamas had told them we all have to get along with each other. He took their questions and went out to a sincere round of applause. I was impressed.

When we got back on the plane, he said he wanted to stop off in his hometown, Plains. He showed me around his residence there, and then around his peanut business. He introduced me to his brother, Billy (his mother was away from home). It was a tour many journalists would be given in the next few years. I wrote an article saying that Carter was aiming to be president, and could well make a good one. Shortly after the article appeared, I met Carter at a Democratic dinner in Washington, and he said he liked what I had written—all but one point. What was that? "Where you said I was trying to run for president." "Aren't you?" "No." Later, when he promised the American people that he would never lie to them, I had reason to question that.

When he did run for president, I flew on his campaign plane, and was impressed all over again. Once, standing in the airplane aisle, someone (I think it was Jim Wooten) asked him how he would differ from a Democratic predecessor, Lyndon Johnson. "I'm not afraid of intellectuals." I believed him. I had read his book, *Why Not the Best?*, which he wrote himself. It had a precision that comes from clear thinking. Later he was asked on the plane, "Why do you keep bringing up religion?" He answered: "I resolved when this campaign began never to bring religion up myself. But you people keep asking me about it. If I don't answer you, you'll say I'm dodging the issue." This was before Reagan and the Moral Majority, and George W. Bush and the Religious Right, made religion a proud part of their campaigns.

Back in 1976, reporters thought an evangelical believer had to be a kook. He was asked if he felt that he was "born again." He said he was, as all Christians must be, since Jesus said (John 3.3), "Except a man be born again, he cannot see the kingdom of God." A leading question from a *Playboy* interviewer provoked Carter to admit that he had experienced lust in his heart. The interviewer did not realize he was just making the evangelical admission that he was a sinner, like all men, and that he was again quoting Jesus, from the Gospel of Matthew (5.28): "whosoever looketh on a woman to lust after her hath committed adultery with her already in his heart." The religious illiteracy of the press was made the basis for charges that Carter was a religious extremist.

While he was campaigning Carter did not announce on his schedule what church he would be going to on Sunday. Those of us who were interested had to follow him to see where he might turn up. Once I was in a small group that sat together in a pew while Carter worshiped in a new church on the campaign trail. The pastor that morning preached from the story at Luke 12.13, where a man asked Jesus to decide on a property dispute with his brother. The preacher said, "Who would dare to bring up such a petty matter with the Lord?" Jody Powell passed a note down the pew from journalist to journalist, with the words: "If Sam Donaldson were following Jesus, he would sure as hell be asked petty questions."

So far from injecting religion into politics, Carter had the historical Baptist belief in a separation of church and state. Roger Williams was one of the earliest proponents of that view, and Baptists were among the strongest supporters of Thomas Jefferson and James Madison, the great champions of religious freedom. When Carter became president, he never had a prayer service in the White House, never invited Billy Graham, the pastor to presidents who would be called in to bless George H. W. Bush's Gulf War. Carter continued to uphold the old Baptist position even after the Southern Baptist Convention broke from its tradition to join the Religious Right. A former president of the Southern Baptists, when he paid a visit to the White House, told Carter that he and his fellow members were praying that the president would give up his "secular humanist" ways.[1]

Carter was the first American president to face up to the energy problems of the world. He responded to the oil crisis of 1979 by cutting back on fuel use in government buildings. He installed solar panels at the White House, promoted wind energy subsidies, and regulated gas consumption in vehicles:

> Between 1973 and 1985, American passenger vehicle mileage went from around 13.5 miles per gallon to 17.5, while light truck mileage increased from 11.6 miles per gallon to 19.5—all of which helped to create a global oil glut from the mid-1980s to the mid-1990s, which not only weakened OPEC but also helped to unravel the Soviet Union, the world's second-largest oil producer.[2]

Yet Carter showed, eventually, that he could be intimidated by intellectuals. When his polls dropped precipitately, he retreated to Camp David and invited in all kinds of professors and pundits. He organized a pep talk to the nation under the bumbling guidance of Patrick Caddell. The address he came down from the mountain to deliver became known as "the malaise speech," though he never used the word "malaise" in it. This, combined with the unflattering picture of him collapsing as he jogged, and with his tale of being assaulted by a rabbit in the water, conveyed a false image of Carter as weak or cowardly. By letting the shah of Iran come to America for medical treatment, he provoked the American hostage crisis in Iran, and his attempt at a rescue raid there was feckless. He boycotted the Moscow Olympics to protest Russia's invasion of Afghanistan. The economy tanked as his term was ending. Thus, despite such achievements as the Panama Canal Treaties and the Camp David Accords, Carter ended up looking provincial, puritanical, and ineffective. His successor, Ronald Reagan, got the credit for the release of the hostages from Iran, a release Carter had prepared. Reagan used Carter's low approval polls (21 percent when he left office) to dismantle Carter's wise energy policy and other governmental regulations.

Out of office, Carter began to recover Americans' respect. I saw two sides of the man at a Mike Mansfield Conference in Montana where we were both on the discussion programs. Speaking to a small audience of students, he was asked how he, who had once been the chief law officer of the nation, could condone the action of his daughter in breaking the law—Amy Carter had been taken to jail for a protest against apartheid held in front of the South African embassy. He answered: "I cannot tell you how proud I am of her. If you students do not express your conscience now, when will you? Later on, you will have many responsibilities—jobs, families, careers. It will get harder and harder to be free to speak out about injustice. Amy was doing that." The students loved him. That was in the afternoon. But at night, in a huge gymnasium, with what looked like half of Montana flooding in, Carter gave a formal speech that was preachy and dull. As he droned on about "agape love," the audience began to stream out at all the doors.

Subsequently, Carter's has been the most successful expresidency of all time. No one else has made such an impact worldwide after leaving the nation's highest office. Thomas Jefferson founded the University of Virginia—but one reason he did that was to baffle the antislavery movement of northern universities. James Madison tried to draft a new constitution for the state of Virginia—but he failed in his compromise measures. Herbert Hoover made important contributions to public life, first by leading the European Food Program in 1947 and then by chairing two Commissions on Organization of the Executive Branch of Government. But Carter's activities dwarf all earlier work by former presidents. He is the only ex-president to be given the Nobel Peace Prize. (Theodore Roosevelt and Barack Obama won the award during their presidencies.) The Carter Center in Atlanta is at the heart of many international negotiations for peace. He has personally overseen the fairness of foreign elections. He has taken an activist role in poverty programs like Habitat for Humanity. He has been a leader in the conversation over moral leadership in politics, arguing that respect for life cannot be restricted to outlawing abortions, gay marriage, and stem cell research.[3] His is a voice of conscience in all nations, not just in ours.

Dukakis

Early in the (early) Iowa primary of 1988 I flew around the state, first with Michael Dukakis, then with his wife Kitty, in progressively smaller prop planes. At the end of one day, when Dukakis had to get back to Massachusetts for some duty as the state's governor, we got on a small Learjet loaned him by a business supporter (there were fewer controls on this back then). Dukakis had only a small staff with him and two journalists. He sat up front with me and the other journalist, David Nyhan of the *Boston Globe*. Nyhan breathed with relief that at last he was on a jet, no matter how small, rather than the prop aircraft we had been riding in short jumps around the state. Dukakis asked why it made a difference to him. Nyhan said the jet made him feel safer, and "I don't want to die." Dukakis said with surprise, "You think of dying?" Nyhan: "Of course. Don't you?" "No, never." I was no longer surprised to hear such an answer from Dukakis. He is the supreme government wonk. If there is no government program against dying, why bother to think about it?

This fit with what he told me when I asked for the book that most influenced him. Unlike many who have to consult their memory or their caution, he answered at once: "Henry Steele Commager's *The American Mind*." It is the most secular account of America one can imagine. To judge from it, no one could imagine religion having any place in American history or culture. It is not surprising that Dukakis was drawn to it. His campaign managers had to remind him that it would be useful for him to remember that he has a Greek heritage, and to start showing up at Greek churches. It was the same pattern observable when another Greek ran for national office. Spiro Agnew, Richard Nixon's vice president, had to resume the name Spiro after being known for most of his adult life as Ted Agnew.

I got what seemed to me the essence of Michael Dukakis when my editor at Simon & Schuster, Alice Mayhew, told me about editing Kitty Dukakis's book during the presidential campaign. Alice called about some changes in the book and got Michael on the line. She asked for Kitty and he told her: "She's in the shower. Call back in thirteen minutes." That attention to detail served him in some ways in his administrative tasks as a governor—and even as a professor—but it did not have the expansive touch of the born politician.

I learned something about Dukakis during the campaign. I took some time off to go to the Kennedy School at Harvard. He had taught there after his failed bid for re-election after a first term as governor. I looked at his student evaluations, and they were excellent. That is far from typical of the politician who turns to the classroom. After George McGovern failed to reach the presidency, my dean at Northwestern considered inviting him to teach a course there. Since I knew McGovern from the 1972 campaign, and from our shared participation in some programs at the Institute for Policy Studies, Dean Weingartner asked if I thought he would make a good visiting professor. I said yes (so much for my academic prescience). McGovern had earned a Ph.D. in history from Northwestern and had been a professor at Dakota Wesleyan University before entering politics. Unlike many politicians, he knew what academic work is all about.

There was intense interest in the course when it was announced. McGovern had run campaigns for the Senate and for president that were well supported on our liberal campus. A huge classroom was set aside for him, and many teaching assistants were happy to sign up to help him with the grading and discussion groups. Despite this large enrollment, McGovern did what many, perhaps most, politicians do when they return to the academy. He began by telling inside stories of the Senate and recounting anecdotes from his various campaigns. But when his stock of tales ran out, he did not know where to go, and students began streaming out of the course. The teaching assistants were left with nothing to do.

Politicians live for contact with people. They lose the gift for contemplation, or research, or simple reading. Being alone with a book is a way to die for many of them. Dukakis was the great exception—and, I presume, still is—since he was always a professor, not a politician.

Bush I

I reported the 1980 campaign for *Time*, and did the cover story on then–vice president Bush. After flying around on his campaign plane, I went to interview Barbara Bush at the vice president's residence. She graciously showed me around the Naval Observatory and we talked of her family. What she most wanted to dwell on was a book she had just completed and admired intensely: Tom Wolfe's *Bonfire of the Vanities*. Then I went to interview Bush at his office in the West Wing of the White House.

After talk of the campaign and of his war service, I asked him what book had influenced him most. He said, "I must admit I'm not much of a reader. I have so many reports and papers to read, I get little time for actual books. Of course, one read the classics in school—*Moby-Dick*. One book made a big impact on me in prep school, *Catcher in the Rye*." Bush graduated from the Phillips Academy in 1942. *Catcher in the Rye* was published in 1951. He was so devoid of personal reading memories that he must have remembered his sons' talk of the novel when they were in prep school.

Before I left, Bush said that next week the Democrats would hold their convention, and he did not want to watch them, so "Bar gave me a book to read instead. But *unhh*, it's so *big*!" Here he mimed taking a book so heavy that his hands sank like a plummet. What was this huge tome? *Bonfire of the Vanities*. Later, after he was elected president, he was asked at times what he was reading. He said he was making his way through *Bonfire of the Vanities*. When George W. Bush became president, his close adviser Karl Rove claimed that he was a voracious reader. Rove was always telling George W. not to be like his father.

NOTES

1. Jimmy Carter, *Our Endangered Values: America's Moral Crisis* (Simon & Schuster, 2005), p. 32.

2. Thomas L. Friedman, *Hot, Flat, and Crowded: Why We Need a Green Revolution—and How It Can Renew America* (Farrar, Straus & Giroux, 2008), p. 14.

3. Carter, op. cit.

10

Clintons

———◆◆❈◆◆———

I was still writing for *Time* when Bill Clinton ran for office. I spent weeks in Little Rock interviewing the Clintons and their acquaintances. I went to see Clinton's mother and brother. I wrote a profile of James Carville for the *New Yorker* after visiting his mother ("Miz Nippy") and sisters in New Orleans. When I had spent some time with Clinton, I got around to asking him for the book that had made the deepest impression on him. He hesitated for a while, and then asked, "What had the most impact on you?" I assured him that was not the game. He is such a politician that I suspected he was taking his time to choose the work that would make me admire him. When he finally came up with a title, I was sure I had been right.

Weeks before, when he asked what I was working on, other than the campaign, I said that I had a long-term project on the *Confessions* of Saint Augustine. So at length he came up with his answer: the *Meditations* of Marcus Aurelius. Dee Dee Myers, his press aide who was sitting in to tape the interview, looked stunned. And sure enough, when we went out of the office, she said to the rest of the staff in the next room, "You'll never guess what he just called his favorite book!" After Clinton was elected, a cheap paperback of the *Meditations* came out with a banner on it saying, "President Clinton's Favorite Book." This should surprise anyone who knows that ascetical treatise, which condemns any yielding to sexual indulgence. At one point it calls intercourse "an internal rubbing with the squirting of slime."

When I asked Hillary Clinton for her favorite book, she did not hesitate for an instant. *"The Brothers Karamazov."* Why? "I read it in high school, and it opened ranges of spirituality I never dreamed of." I came to know her fairly well, and to like her a lot. She drove me around Little Rock. We ate lunches at a restaurant and in the governor's mansion. She has a wonderful sense of humor, along with a gift (also shared by Barack Obama) of imitating the voices of people when she tells stories, as when she told me of a case she took when she was teaching at the University of Arkansas in Fayetteville. She did pro bono work off campus, and one day she got a phone call from a small town in the north Arkansas hills. There was a black woman being held there without legal representation. Could she come? Her fellow professor and future husband, Bill, had their one car that day, so she got a law student to take her to the town in his truck.

Arrived, she found that the woman was a black lay preacher who shouted about Jesus on the street corner of the little hamlet. Her arrest was for disturbing the peace. Hillary went to talk to the judge, then visited the woman. She asked where she came from. "California." "Don't you figure there are souls to be saved in California?" Oh, yeah. "If I got you a ticket back to California, would you want to go there?" Yeah. Hillary went to the judge and said, "If I get the money to send her to California, will you drop the charges against her?" He said yes. What fascinated me was the way she spoke in character, both as the judge and as the woman preacher. It is a natural tendency that got her into trouble when she said she was not just standing by her man, like Tammy Wynette—people thought her accent was mocking Wynette.

Her humor came out when she told me how Bill and Taylor Branch worked for the McGovern campaign in Texas. She later joined them, taking leave from her work in Washington, but she had not gone there yet. Bill's director in Texas was Gary Hart. At one point Bill said he wanted to take a weekend off to go see his girlfriend in Washington. Hart was indignant: "How can you think of girlfriends in the heat of a campaign?" Considering Hart's hanky-panky in the midst of his own later campaign for the presidency, this amused Hillary no end. (She probably found it less funny after the Monica Lewinsky episode.)

We talked about religion, of which she is a sincere practitioner. And she was also humble. She told me she did not like her speaking style, and asked me what I would do to improve my speaking if I had trouble with it. "I suppose," I said, "I would pay attention to good speakers and try to figure out how they do it." Like who? she asked. I said I thought black Baptists were the best speakers alive, but she could not imitate them without looking as if she caricatured them. Who else? she asked. I suggested Mario Cuomo, and she later told me she was paying attention to his style.

When the Clintons were in the White House, Hillary invited me to the Millennium dinners she threw to prepare for the year 2000, but they all took place on days when I had an afternoon class, so I did not get to any of them. Then along came the Monica scandal. When Bill finally owned up to his dalliance, Walter

Isaacson, then the editor of *Time,* called and asked me if I could write something about it overnight. I agreed to, and wrote that Clinton should resign and turn the White House over to his vice president, Al Gore—otherwise he would spend the rest of his term fending off legal and political challenges. When I did this, my wife said, "You know, he is supposed to be giving you a medal in a few weeks" (the National Endowment for the Humanities award). I said I knew.

At the NEH event, we met with the Clintons before going out into the Rose Garden for the ceremony. I did not know how the Clintons would treat me. I stuck out my hand to shake Hillary's. She said: "Don't I get a hug?" As we hugged, she said, "You're sitting next to me at dinner tonight." Bill told me he had been reading Saint Augustine's *Confessions.* I don't think this was because he remembered my interest in the book. I had read that the preachers brought in to counsel him in his remorseful period after Monica were giving him penitential readings.

I knew the White House speechwriter who had composed the citation Clinton had to read before giving me the medal—Ted Widmer, who was serving a year there after getting his doctorate from Harvard. He told me it was a flattering document, as all such texts must be, and he was not sure that Clinton would read it as he wrote it, after I had called for his resignation. In fact, Clinton soldiered through it as written—but he stopped to interject one comment. Widmer had written something about my having incisive things to say across a broad spectrum of subjects. Here Clinton paused and said, "Sometimes I have a little problem with that"—which was, of course, the perfect way to handle the situation.

That night at dinner, I said to Hillary, "You are a poor planner. You have me at the same table with Gregory Peck. You could have put him beside you." No, she said, she had planned well. "This way I get to talk with you and look at him."

My wife and I were invited to one more dinner at the White House. This one occurred after George Bush's election but before his inauguration. Hillary said, "This time Bill gets you." I was at the president's round table, and was conducted over to it before most people came in. I found my place card, and read the name on the next card: Stewart. My friend Susan Manilow, who was to sit across from me, came around and looked at it. "Who is that?" I asked. "Must be Martha," she said. And it was I asked Martha Stewart, when she arrived, to critique the table setting. "Oh, cut it out," she said. After we sat down, she brought up Greek and Latin books. She knew I am a classicist from her son-in-law, a lawyer with a great interest in the classics. She told me she had bought him the Loeb Library as a gift. I was stunned—there are several hundred bilingual volumes of classical authors in the Loeb Library. After the dinner was over, he wandered by from a different table and I said I had heard about the Loeb—she nudged me. The gift, not yet given, was supposed to be a surprise. With a blank look, he said, "What?" I improvised in panic: "We were talking about the Leopold-Loeb trial at dinner." He was still looking blank when he went off. I told her, "I hope I didn't blow it for you." "No," she said, "you just confused him. At least, you confused the hell out of me."

Stewart was seated to my right. To my left, three seats over from the president, was singer Denise Rich, whom I had never heard of. At one point in the meal, she said, "You know,

Nostradamus predicted the victory of Bush." I nodded, to avoid getting further into that wacky subject. "What did she say?" Stewart whispered to me. "That Nostradamus predicted the election." She laughed: "I don't think Nostradamus is in the Loeb Library."

I learned who Denise Rich was after the Clintons left the White House. The pardon for her ex-husband Marc was the last scandal of the Clinton years. Some reporters who found out the seating arrangement at Clinton's table on that night called me up to ask if the pardon was discussed at the meal. I said, "Of course not." Clinton came around after dinner and talked to Rich and me, but only about the election Gore had just lost (his was a non-Nostradamus version of it).

I kept my record for political prescience when talk arose about Hillary running for the Senate in New York after leaving Washington. I told her friend Sidney Blumenthal that I did not think she would (or should). I felt she needed some time to get free of the White House controversies. When she did run, I thought she would lose. In 2008 I was asked if she would be appointed as Obama's vice president if he won the primaries. I said no. Then, would she be secretary of state? No. My predicting record cannot match that of Nostradamus.

11

Jack

———◆━▶◄◆▶◄◆———

I was often an outsider in my family. Neither of my parents went to college or read books. I mentioned earlier that they felt my reading was abnormal. My mother humored me without understanding my bookworm ways. I admired my father, Jack, and I didn't. I disliked him, and I didn't. I pleaded with my mother not to remarry him after a sad and draining divorce. But she did, and I was finally glad. He was hard to resist.

After that remarriage, we were vacationing on Michigan's Mackinac Island, my parents and my own young family. Out in a field, my father saw a horse roaming free. He had ridden horses as a boy in Arizona and Cuba, where his father was an engineer, but he was now in his forties and the horse had no bridle or saddle. Nonetheless, he tried to vault onto its back. It easily flicked him aside. I checked to see if he had broken anything, and told him, "Don't try that again." Of course he did, unsuccessfully. As he told me several times, "There is no such word as 'cannot' in the Wills dictionary."

One of his many business ventures was a debt-consolidation scheme, when that was a new invention to keep creditors from garnishing wages. Jack would collect his clients' monthly wages and portion them out to creditors. One man kept trying to evade my father, to keep his wages. As Jack was pestering him, the man hit him. My father had been a Golden Gloves boxer, a college boxing coach, and camp champion in the army during World War II. He rarely resisted a fight. But this man was so big that he easily beat my father. Nonetheless, Jack went back and back to him, getting beaten every time, until the man finally said, "Shit, Jack, I have to pay you or kill you—so I'll pay you." They became good friends after that, and the man was at Jack's funeral years later (where he reminded me that he had not killed him).

Jack was small and wiry—he admired actors and athletes who were just as small, Bob Steele in movie westerns, James Cagney in crime films, Alan Ladd in mysteries. Jack was a natural athlete who lettered in four sports at his high school (Georgia Military Academy). I read his school paper, which said he did everything on the football field, quarterbacking, punting, drop-kicking (when there was still such a thing). He played without a helmet, claiming that a helmet reduced his peripheral vision. Later, he refused to wear seat belts in a car, claiming that his quick reflexes would let him dodge any trouble.

He won golf prizes until his street fights broke so many bones in his hand that his grip was hard to manage—it bothered him that I hated golf, thinking it a waste of golden daylight hours when I could be reading. His older brother, Bob, with whom he never got along, knew that he was not only a good golfer but a natural teacher (a thing he proved in his days as a boxing coach), and Bob came back from California to Michigan to take golf lessons from him. I was sent out to shag balls until descending darkness made the balls unfindable. Jack's natural teaching skills made him show me how to serve a tennis ball and punt a football, the only (isolated) sport skills I ever acquired. He dearly wanted to show me how to drive a golf ball, but I resisted that evil knowledge.

Jack hoped to play football for Georgia Tech, but he was too small to get a scholarship when he graduated from high school in the depths of the Depression (1934). My mother, pregnant with me, had to drop out of high school, and Jack could not find work in the hard-hit South. My Irish grandmother was a locally famed baker, and for a while he peddled her bread from door to door. But then he headed north looking for a job. He had a small used convertible his father had given him. My mother was in the front seat, his Great Dane was in the backseat (Danes were a fixture in his life), and I, newborn, was in a dresser-drawer crib in the rumble seat. When he rammed into a halted car, the drawer was jolted out onto the road behind, but I rode it out safely.

Women always loved Jack, including my mother's mother, Rose Collins. Rose's own Irish mother (a Meehan) was crippled and could never leave the second-floor flat they lived in. When my father came to visit, he always carried Grandmother Meehan downstairs and took her for rare outings in the convertible, to a park or a movie or the church bingo game. That endeared him forever to Rose. In 1937, the Collinses had moved from Atlanta to Louisville when the great flood of the Ohio River hit Kentucky. Jack, then working in Michigan, instantly rented an outboard-motor boat, hitched it to the back of his car, and drove to Louisville. Parking the car at the edge of the flood, he took the boat to get Grandmother Meehan and my mother's two sisters (as much as the boat would carry). After taking them to safety, he went back and got my grandparents, Rose and Con.

This Irish side of the family welcomed Jack warmly into its midst. His own family, the English Willses from Virginia, had aristocratic pretensions—he was christened John Hopkins Wills, named (approximately) after the founder of the university. His prim mother, a Christian Scientist, always favored the older, more staid son, Bob. Jack's father, after whom I am named, was a bit of a rogue and always favored Jack, who was a lifelong hunting buddy. When Jack, at GMA, climbed up to the tower of a nearby girls' school and rang its bell in the middle of the night, the GMA authorities wrote a harsh letter to Garry Wills threatening Jack with expulsion. His father telegraphed back, "I did not know I was sending you to a kindergarten. Come home immediately." That made the school back off. Later, when the two were hunting, they circled a copse and Garry inadvertently sprayed Jack with shotgun pellets. My father was rushed to the hospital to have the pellets removed. When he took his army physical in World War II, an X-ray showed he still had a pellet in his jaw.

My mother put up with my father's affairs for years, even offering to raise one of the children born to a mistress. But one night as I was up reading, I heard her weeping as she took a phone call from a young woman's mother, who said that he had begun an affair with her daughter, who worked as a waitress in the hunting lodge where Jack was staying with his father. That was the end, she thought. And though Jack pleaded with her not to divorce him, even getting her priest to say Catholics cannot divorce, no matter how a husband may stray, she threw him out of the house. My younger sister did not realize what was happening, and resented my mother for turning him away. My mother, with saintly forbearance, did not tell her the real reason—and when, years later, my sister found out the truth, she was so angry at Jack that I had a hard time persuading her to come to his funeral.

Jack went with the young waitress to California, where she became a television model—they were married on the TV wedding show where she worked. In 1951, when I graduated from high school, a friend and I qualified for the national finals of an oratory contest in Los Angeles. We drove out there in the car my friend had been given as a graduation present, and we stayed with my father, his wife, and his young daughter. When my friend went back east, my father asked me to stay and work for his new business, selling ranges and refrigerators. He showed me around Los Angeles, and tried to dissuade me from going back to the Midwest, where I was scheduled to enter a Jesuit seminary.

Jack owned a vacant lot next to his appliance store. It was too overgrown and briary to be mowed, so he decided to burn the brush away—always a dangerous thing in California. On the other side of the lot was a fancy restaurant, where patrons could catch fish in a stocked pond for their meal. The fire began to race toward the restaurant, and Jack gave me an ineffectual hose to head it off while he went to call the fire department. Luckily, the fire engines arrived just in time. Another close call for Jack.

One day, I had to deliver a refrigerator across town while he was staying for an appointment with buyers in the store. He did not yet have a delivery truck, so he hitched a trailer behind his car and sent me off to deliver the appliance. I was seventeen and had not had my driver's license for long. Jack, in his teacher mode, gave me a quick lesson on how to back up a trailer (turn one way to go the other way). How, I asked, was I to unload the refrigerator? He said, "Find someone standing by and offer him five dollars to help you." "Cannot" was a word absent from Jack's dictionary. Years later, when he had remarried my mother, he bought a lot next to their house on Lake Lansing and turned it into a remunerative garbage dump (to the disgust of lake property owners). He had an old used earthmover to bulldoze the garbage with, and he gave me a quick lesson on how to drive it. It brought back memories of my first navigation of the Los Angeles streets with his trailer.

Jack was an ingenious inventor of business schemes. Unfortunately, he was easily bored with them after they began to make money. Also, he was a heavy gambler. On the night before he went into the army, he got into a high-stakes poker game at the Elks Club, and I, as an eight-year-old, watched him lose all his ready cash. My mother had to rent our best house and move into a rental one that we had lived in when Jack first reached Michigan. That first house was large, but he met its monthly payments by renting its upstairs floors to students from nearby Albion College. The student boarders adopted me as a kind of mascot (I was four at the time). They rode me around on their bikes, taught me to tie my shoelaces, and made me think the life of a student the most wonderful thing imaginable.

Jack was coaching the college boxers and judging Golden Gloves matches (where he took me to ringside seats). Jack, like the rest of my family, southern on both sides, was a racist. He always bet against Joe Louis, and when I got a little older I made money from those bets. He claimed that the white men who went against Louis lost only because they tried to hit him in the head—blacks have iron heads—instead of hacking him down with midsection blows.

Jack was fearless—but that was because he felt he could never die. He was superstitious about hospitals. He did not want to admit to human limits. To his credit, he went to the hospital and gave my mother a blood transfusion when she bled badly after delivering me—she was a teenager and I had weighed almost twelve pounds. But he could not bring himself to visit my mother after she went into a coma in her final bout with cancer. Not because he did not love her—he just could not face the thought of losing her. My sister and I had to make the decision to remove her life support after the doctor said she could not revive.

Jack had an infectious sense of fun, and an extraordinary resilience after business setbacks. He always invented some way out of his troubles. At his funeral, the man who'd said he had to pay him or kill him came up to me as the military salute was being fired, over the hill, dim in the wind, a faint pop-pop-pop. "Leave it to Jack," the man said, "to get the popcorn concession at his own funeral."

One of the reasons I am a conservative is that I do not believe that "cannot" should be removed from the dictionary. A recognition of limits is important to human life, and especially to human politics. On the other hand, a defiance of human limits is an exhilarating prospect, and it explains why Jack fascinated people. There is, I suppose, a little bit of Jack in me—very little—that I would not remove, even if I could.

12

Studs

————— ◆◆✕◆◆ —————

In 2008, Studs Terkel had a new book coming out—the fourth one he had produced since turning ninety.[1] I was writing a review of the new book when his son called to tell me he had died (at age ninety-six). Terkel's astonishing late productivity came from what would seem a crippling development, the fact that he lost most of his hearing during those late years, despite the best efforts of doctors and hearing-aid technicians. Bad as this would be for any of us, it was a special blow to Terkel, whose specialty was hearing others tell about themselves. I had been in cabs with him and wondered at his ability to elicit the driver's whole life story before we reached our destination.

It was a gift that came from empathy, curiosity, and a willingness to let others express their views, even when Terkel did not share them—as when he interviewed the pilot who dropped the bomb on Hiroshima, or a member of the Ku Klux Klan. On his gift for empathetic listening he built a literature of oral histories and radio interviews with people famous and obscure, all of them unusually willing to reveal themselves in intimate ways. He gave his vast trove of tapes to the Chicago History Museum, where the interviews will be listened to in perpetuity.

(Where else can you hear the voice of Dorothy Parker being witty or Zero Mostel being explosive—Mostel is the only one I ever heard call him "Studsy.")

When he was deprived of his ability to listen to others, he dug into his own memories, his vast experience, his range of acquaintances (many then dead), and his observations of the worlds of politics, music, theater, and urban life. With the help of his longtime assistant at WFMT radio, Sydney Lewis, and the encouragement of his longtime editor, Andre Schiffrin of the New Press, Terkel took his isolation from sound as an opportunity to write more than he had in any other part of his life.

The wonder is that he was not really isolated. I had seen him, in earlier days, walk along the street in Chicago and be mobbed by people wanting to talk with him. He welcomed them all, and made slow if any progress to wherever he was going. But even when he was mainly immobilized in his Prairie School house in the northern part of Chicago, the world beat a path to his door. People still wanted to talk with him, even if they had to shout at close range and repeat themselves. In his later months, streams of people came to draw on his genial memories. Director Peter Sellars asked to see him when he brought *Doctor Atomic* to the Lyric Opera. Mos Def, the actor and hip-hop artist, who wants to do radio interviews modeled on those of Terkel, brought his musician father, who had played with some of Terkel's friends in the folk music world. Neal Baer, the philanthropist and producer of *Law & Order: SVU,* who was doing a book on storytelling as a lifesaver, wanted to consult the practiced storyteller. Old friends dropped in whenever they could—Garrison Keillor,

David Schwimmer, Jules Feiffer, and Roger Ebert before his own illness kept him away. Terkel was lively to the end, and offered them all, whatever the time of day, "a little touch" of Scotch or their preference.

Though Terkel was born in New York and only came to Chicago when he was eight, he was totally identified with the city. Once, when he was in his eighties, I drove him from his home toward the downtown Loop. As Lake Michigan and the city skyline came into view, he said, "I would have been dead long ago but for this place." He was a Chicago institution, one who outlived several Chicago institutions who once ranked with him. In later parts of the twentieth century, he was paired with radio host Irv Kupcinet, tough columnist Mike Royko, and novelist Nelson Algren. Earlier, in midcentury, he was part of the pioneering Chicago School of Television, a relaxed and improvisational continuation of Chicago radio styles. *Kukla, Fran and Ollie* and *Garroway at Large* were picked up by New York syndicates, but Terkel's show, *Studs' Place*, ran only two seasons in the early fifties before the blacklist forced him off the air. The show was about a diner, with a stock company of waiters and customers somewhat like those in the later television show *Cheers*. There was nothing political about *Studs' Place* but the red-checked tablecloths, like the red-checked shirts and red socks and ties that Terkel always wore as a sign of his radical sympathies. (At his ninetieth birthday celebration, people wore red-checked cloth patches on their shirts and blouses, and the set of *Studs' Place*—red-checked tablecloths and all—was reproduced on the stage of the Chicago History Museum.)

The fact that Terkel went early into television was not surprising. He grew up in his mother's boarding hotel, which often had second-string show business people staying there. He was a super in operas as a boy. He acted in local theater groups and on radio soap operas, sometimes with Nancy Reagan's mother, Edith Luckett. His last book, *P.S.*, tells how on *Ma Perkins* the actors were held verbatim to the script, leaving full time for the all-important commercials. One day a snowstorm delayed arrival of the scripts, so they had to improvise, with no real experience of winging it. Taking a cue from the weather, the cast confected the story of a storm. The young actor playing Ma Perkins's son ventured: "Ma, walk behind me, I'll break wind for you."

When Terkel interviewed Leonard Bernstein on his long-running radio show, Bernstein said, "You probably never heard of Marc Blitzstein." Terkel said, "What do you mean? I acted in *The Cradle Will Rock*." "You did? What part?" "The newspaper editor." "Oh, typecasting. Sing the editor's song." Terkel began singing it and Bernstein chimed in, before going on to sing almost every song in the opera. Bernstein did not know that Terkel had interviewed four actors from *Cradle*'s famous first performance, when Orson Welles took the locked-out cast to a deserted theater on the night of the premiere.

Terkel even acted in a couple of movies. In *Eight Men Out* (1988) he played a reporter (again, typecasting). In *The Dollmaker* (1984) he had a bit part as a cabdriver. On a photograph of him in the role Jane Fonda wrote, "What a thrill to be upstaged by you, Studs." But after Terkel had delivered his few lines from the driver's seat of the cab, the director told him to drive off.

Terkel had to admit that he did not know how to drive, and a stuntman was quickly recruited to take the shot. "I'm the only bit player who had an understudy," Terkel liked to say in later years. He did not want to drive all by himself. He regularly took the bus to work, talking with whoever was near him. I first heard from him in the 1970s, when he wrote to me in Baltimore that he liked some article of mine so much that he photocopied it at work and passed it out to everyone on the bus when he went home.

A boy who lived across the street from him said Studs would get off the bus and come down the street still talking away with his imagined audience. Once, when a married couple waiting for the bus complained about "liberal labor unions," Studs asked the man, "Do you work more than eight hours a day?" When he said no, Studs answered, "Why do you think that is? The unions, that's why." He asked the woman if she voted. When she said yes, he said, "Why do you think that is? The liberals, that's why."

Terkel did not originally intend to be an actor or a radio interviewer or a liberal agitator. To follow the example of his lawyer hero Clarence Darrow, he graduated from the University of Chicago Law School, but few firms were hiring Jews in the Depression (Terkel's parents were Jewish immigrants from Bialystok in Ukraine), so he applied for a position with the FBI. Only when he was turned down by the FBI (he thought it was for being a Jew) did he start a scrambling Depression existence as actor, disc jockey, sports reporter, and announcer at musical events. In the latter role, he became a close friend of singer Mahalia Jackson. In the McCarthy period, a television station demanded that he sign a loyalty oath. After Terkel refused, and was on the point of being fired, Mahalia told the station, "If Studs goes, I go."

Terkel found his real métier when he began his long run of interview shows on WFMT, a radio station devoted mainly to classical music but also to folk music, jazz, and drama. Terkel interviewed one person or group for an hour every weekday, and the show went on for forty-five years. His interviews had an extraordinary range. Actors were amazed at his encyclopedic knowledge of the theater. The Lyric Opera regularly sent him visiting singers to be interviewed, and Terkel became a friend of regulars in Chicago like Tito Gobbi. Folksingers showed up often. Authors all noted how closely he had read and marked up their books. Terkel used appropriate recorded interludes keyed to the contents of the book. For my *Lincoln at Gettysburg* he played Civil War songs and Orson Welles reciting the Gettysburg Address—no surprise there. But I was astonished when I went on to talk about my biography of Saint Augustine and he played Ambrosian chant—he had read in my book that Augustine was baptized by Ambrose, but somehow he knew on his own that Ambrose had introduced a new musical style in Milan.

Terkel began adding a second layer to his marathon of interviews in 1966, when Andre Schiffrin suggested that he use his technique to create a composite picture of a city made up of interviews with all types of its citizens. The result was *Division Street: America* (1967), the first in a series of oral histories—of the Depression (*Hard Times*, 1970), of labor (*Working*, 1974), of aspirations (*American Dreams*, 1980), of World War II (*"The Good War,"*

1985), of racial relations (*Race*, 1992), of youth (*Coming of Age*, 1995), of performing (*The Spectator*, 1999), of dying (*Will the Circle Be Unbroken?*, 2001), of aging (*Hope Dies Last*, 2003). These and others were all published by Schiffrin, at first for Pantheon. When Schiffrin broke with Pantheon, Terkel imitated his old friend Mahalia Jackson: "If Andre goes, Studs goes." Terkel became a mainstay of Schiffrin's New Press.

The printed interviews do not reveal the ways Terkel established a rapport with his subjects. But listening to the full tapes shows what connections he forged with his subjects. When a woman said she was "just a housewife" who never accomplished anything, unlike her daughter, Terkel replied that her daughter's career showed what a great mother she had been, and the woman began reflecting on the good things in her life. People, especially working-class people, left his interviews feeling good about themselves. The maddest I ever saw Terkel was when he remembered the way a waitress was derided in the movie *Five Easy Pieces.*

Some objected to interviews in his books—to his sympathy with gays, to the occasionally rough language of his interlocutors. *Working* was banned from certain high schools because it contains the word "fuck." An irate letter writer got so spluttering that he misquoted the book's title as *Working Studs.* Studs went to one such school and explained that the word was used by a firefighter who had just been told that his friend and fellow fireman had been killed. He said it was the only way the man could express the depth of his anguish. He made the person's plight so vivid that the school rescinded the ban. The Terkel talent for instant connection with people showed up in the oddest ways. Once he got a wrong number on the phone and struck up a long conversation with a young boy he had never met, finding out about the boy's whole school record and future plans.

This ability to connect was proved when his home was burgled. As he later told the story, Terkel's wife, Ida, was ill, so she lay on the couch downstairs rather than going up to the bedroom. Terkel had been in a chair reading to her till she went to sleep, and he turned off the light. A burglar came in through the window, not realizing the room was occupied. When Terkel turned on the light, the startled man demanded money. Terkel talked in a soothing voice and pointed out his sick wife. He told the man all he had was two twenties in his wallet. The man took them and was about to leave, but Terkel said he needed money for a cab, to go in the morning to buy medicine for his wife. The man looked at her and gave back one of the twenties. Terkel said, "Thank you"; the man said, "You're welcome," and started to go back out the window. Terkel said, "You don't have to do that," and conducted him over to the front door. The man went out, turned, and said, "Thank you," and Terkel said, "You're welcome." We needed a Terkel to be conducting our peace talks in the Middle East.

Terkel and such old friends as the medical reformer Quentin Young and the civil rights lawyer Leon Despres called themselves "old lefties." They fought the first Mayor Daley's Chicago regime with high spirits. Theirs was not the bitter or recriminating leftism of a Noam Chomsky. When they were together, I heard mainly laughter, and the mutual teasing that prevents self-importance. Their kind of lefty was E. Y. "Yip" Harburg.

When Terkel interviewed him, they reminisced less about their blacklisting than about Harburg's high-spirited song lyrics for *The Wizard of Oz* or *Finian's Rainbow*. Terkel especially liked such lines as "When I'm not facing the face that I fancy, I fancy the face I face."

Terkel and his like were labor-union liberals. At age ninety-one Terkel took the bullhorn at a strike meeting of local hotel workers. He would never cross a picket line. When I crossed a teaching assistants' strike line to give a series of lectures at Yale, I was careful not to let Terkel know. He had been active in Henry Wallace's 1948 campaign for president. In 2000, remembering work with Ralph Nader in his earlier campaigns for car safety, Terkel spoke at a rally for Nader as president. We had knock-down-drag-out arguments over that, and Terkel told a shared friend that he was afraid I would never speak to him again if Nader caused Gore to lose (as he did). But Terkel did not in the end vote for Nader, and Illinois was unaffected by Nader's disastrous interventions.

I could never stay mad at Terkel, if only because of Ida. In 1939 Terkel married Ida Goldberg, a social worker, tiny, pretty, soft-voiced, maternal, a pacifist more radical than he, and far more practical. They had a car because she knew how to drive— and how to pay the bills and organize the house. She had been to more antiwar demonstrations than Terkel—she was arrested in Washington, D.C., in 1972. When I first went to her home in 1980, she said, "It's good to see you again, Garry—we went to jail together."

In 1969, when Fred Hampton of the Black Panthers was murdered in his apartment by the Chicago police, it was feared there would be further assaults on the apartment, so she and some women friends set up a card table on the building's porch and provided a human shield for those inside. When my wife and I took Ida down to march in the Loop against the Gulf War in 1990, people kept coming up and greeting her with memories of other demonstrations they had been in with her.

When Studs and Ida got their FBI files, he was jealous that her file was thicker than his. But hers was the first approval he sought after giving a speech. "How did I do, Ida?" he would ask. She would say, "You did fine, Louis," and he would beam. (She was the only one alive who called him by his birth name—as a young man he acquired the name Studs from his admiration of James T. Farrell's Studs Lonigan novels.) Ida died in 1999, at eighty-seven, in the sixtieth year of her marriage to Studs. His friends feared that he would no longer be able to function, from grief and from loss of her management skills. But their son and a number of friends filled in with an attempt to be surrogate Idas. He put her cremated ashes on the windowsill of the room where she lay when the burglar entered, saving them to be mixed with his when he died.

He was much acclaimed in his life—with honorary college degrees (his commencement addresses were a hit), with a Pulitzer Prize, a National Book Award for lifetime achievement, the National Humanities Medal bestowed on him by President Clinton, the Elijah Parish Lovejoy Award, the Dayton Literary Peace Award, and the Prix Italia (for a documentary on the Cuban Missile Crisis). He wore his honors lightly, as if not wanting anything to set him apart from the people he met every day on the bus, or the schoolchildren he used to visit, or his myriad friends from all walks of life. He lit up in the company of his fellow beings, and positively glowed when a friend came into view.

It was fun just entering his house. He would whoop with welcome, using his favorite word, "Fan-TAS—tic." Always pronounced that way. When he was in the hospital after a neck operation, he introduced me to his nurse. "She's fantastic." When he read something I wrote he would call me up to say that it was fantastic. He was a virtuoso of wonder, forever grateful and generous. He loved to do things for people. He always brought women flowers. When I was in the hospital, he sent me the complete recordings of Hoagy Carmichael—an indication of his eclectic taste as well as of his generosity.

He drew people out by appreciating them. And what he drew out was the best in people. They were embarrassed not to live up to his admiration of them. It is said that artists keep an inner child alive in themselves. Studs did that. One of my favorite images of him is his practicing to throw out the opening pitch at a Chicago White Sox game. He got his across-the-street neighbor Laura Watson, a good athlete, to come over to the lot beside his house and catch his practice pitches. Laura says he had all the "business" down pat, adjusting his baseball hat (the wrong hat—Chicago Cubs; he had not had time to get the White Sox one), shaking off a catcher's signal, pretending to "chaw" tobacco. One day, he knocked on the Watsons' door and asked Bob, her husband, "Can Laura come out to play?" Bob said it was raining out. "Yeah," Studs answered, "but not very hard." Besides, Bob went on, it was Mother's Day and their children were coming. "Oh, all right," said

Studs, downcast as any kid would be if told he could not go out and play.

Studs might have been childlike, but he was not naive. He could size up phonies or ideologues, the greedy and selfish politicians. Another favorite image I have of him occurred at Northwestern University, where he was getting an honorary degree. I was his faculty presenter, so we put on our robes together. Across the room, also robing up, was another honoree of the day, Judge Richard Posner, the man who thinks the law should follow marketplace rules, reducing everything to right-wing economics. We went over to say hello, and Studs asked if he still taught at Studs's alma mater, the University of Chicago Law School. Yes, Posner answered. Studs inquired what he had taught during the semester that just ended. Already by then Studs was getting so deaf that he often heard what he expected to hear, not what was actually said. So when Posner said that he had taught "Evidence," Studs leaned over, hand to ear, and said, "Avarice?" The British have a term, "gobsmacked," that perfectly describes Posner's expression at that point.

On a nippy May morning in 2009, his son, Dan, and a small party of his friends buried his and Ida's ashes under a tree that his friends had planted earlier in Bughouse Square, the Chicago equivalent of London's Hyde Park Speakers' Corner, where the young Studs had heard radicals denounce the powerful. He knew this was where he would be most at peace, and had asked that we bring him to this as his Chicago home. We knew that we would never again cross the door of his home, hear his whoop of welcome, and be offered "a little touch." Life has not been quite the same since.

NOTES

   1. *Hope Dies Last* (2003), *And They All Sang* (2005), *Touch and Go* (2007), *P.S.* (2008). He wrote six books after his eighty-sixth birthday—add *The Spectator* (1999) and *Will the Circle Be Unbroken?* (2001) to the last four.

13

Bill

———◆▸◦◂◆———

Hour by hour, day by day, Bill Buckley was just an exciting person to be around, especially when he was exhilarated by his love of sailing. He could turn any event into an adventure, a joke, a showdown. He loved risk. I saw him time after time rush his boat toward a harbor, sails flying, only to swerve and drop sail at the last moment. For some on the pier, looking up to see this large yacht bearing down on them, it was a heart-stopping moment. To add to the excitement, Bill was often standing on the helmsman's seat, his hands hanging from the backstays, steering the wheel with his foot, in a swashbuckling pose. (He claimed he saw the berth better from up there.)

I saw once how important were his swift reflexes on the boat. We had set out for a night sail on the ocean, and Bill's Yale friend Van Galbraith—later President Reagan's ambassador to France—had got tipsy from repeated Tia Marias in his coffee after dinner. He fell overboard while the boat was under full sail. In a flash Bill threw out the life preserver with a bright light on it, and called for us to bring the boat about. We circled back toward Galbraith, found him in the darkness, and fished him up. It was a scary moment, one that only Bill's cool rapidity kept from being a tragic one.

Bill liked to sail so much that he kept a little two-person Sun-fish boat at his home in Stamford, to take out for an hour or two on a nice day. He taught me the rudiments of sailing on it. On his big boats—the *Panic,* the *Suzy Wong,* the *Cyrano*—he let me take the helm, instructing me to watch the nylon "telltale" on the shroud, even letting me come about (I tell you he loved risk). I got to like sailing so much I bought my own small boat (a Snipe) to sail on Lake Lansing—my son later sailed it on Lake Michigan. Once, sailing out with Bill from Miami, when we were hit by a storm, he congratulated me on the skills I had learned from him.

Bill wrote the way he sailed, taking chances. Once he called me up to ask about some new papal pronouncement. He had got into trouble with fellow Catholics by criticizing papal encyclicals, and I had become a kind of informal adviser on Catholic matters. The statement at issue that day was obscure in its immediate sense. He wanted to launch an instant attack on it. I asked why he did not wait to see what impact it would have. "Why not wait? Because I don't have *falsos testes.*" He was referring to an earlier discussion, when he asked whether even papal defenders admit the pontiff can err. I said that medieval commentators claimed this could happen if the pope was given imperfect evidence (*propter falsos testes*). He asked, "Isn't *testis* [testifier] the same word in Latin as testicle?" Yes. That was all the warrant he needed.

He was always ready to plunge in. Another time he called me and asked, "Have you ever heard of Joe Nuh-*math*?" This was when everybody had heard of the way Joe *Nay*-math won the 1969 Super Bowl as quarterback for the New York Jets. Bill had never heard the name pronounced, he just read it in an editor's letter asking him to write about the man. I told him how Namath had beat my hero, John Unitas, in the Super Bowl. There were large gaps in Bill's knowledge of popular culture, especially of popular sports. His father once wrote to Bill's future father-in-law, complaining that he had tried for years, without success, to interest his son in ordinary games—golf or tennis or team sports. But Bill had a relish only for solo performances—sailing, skiing, horseback riding, or flying an airplane. I asked if Bill was going to write about Namath. Yes. "That should be an interesting interview." He said, "Oh, I don't have time to learn enough about football to interview him." He wrote the piece by comparing Namath to something he did know: the record of a famous bullfighter.

Another time I was on Bill's boat racing to Bermuda. We saw on the horizon a huge shape like an island—it was a World War II battleship taken out of mothballs and put on a shakedown cruise before being sent to the Vietnam War, a breathtaking sight from our lower vantage point on the water. Bill could not resist hailing it on the radio, though it was against racing rules to radio except in an emergency. When we reached Bermuda, Bill was disqualified. One of the other boats had heard his conversation with the battleship and reported him. He said it was worth it. He reminded me of one of Wodehouse's blithe young men—Psmith, say, or Piccadilly Jim—who act forever on impulse.

He took risks even in routine and mundane ways. One night, after dinner at his town house in Manhattan, he wanted to continue our conversation, so instead of calling me a cab to take me back to my hotel, he gave me a ride on his motorbike. It was the law in New York that bikers wear a helmet, so we were stopped by a policeman—neither of us was helmeted. When the cop recognized him, he let us go with just a warning, since Bill was popular with cops for opposing police review boards. Needless to say, the next time he gave me a ride, there were still no helmets.

It is amazing that Bill's risks did not end his life. At Yale he secretly learned to fly, and bought a small plane with some classmates, not letting his father know about it. He landed the plane at his sister Maureen's prep school in a spectacular visit. Then, on the day when he passed some college tests, he took the plane out for a celebratory spin, all by himself. He had been up the night before cramming for his exams, and he fell asleep at the controls. Luckily he woke in time to bring the plane down. A great career might have ended before it began.

For a while I was Bill's designated biographer. A shared friend of ours, Neil McCaffrey, commissioned the book for his new publishing venture, Arlington House. Bill approved the idea because, like many celebrities, he was constantly pestered by people wanting to interview him for books or magazines. With me as his chosen scribe, he could turn them down by saying he was already committed. I recorded many hours of tapes with him, his wife, his siblings, his friends, for the project, before giving it up over political disagreements and returning the advance to Neil.

Bill was stunningly candid on these tapes, so much so that I, like many people close to him, came to feel I should protect him from his own reckless truthfulness. He was too trusting of people he liked. He set up a former boat boy in a partnership to buy radio stations, and afterward found that his young partner had bilked him. He argued for the innocence of a prisoner who wrote him winning letters, and worked to have Edgar Smith released, only to see the man be convicted again of kidnapping and attempted murder.

Some of the things Bill told me at the time I have never repeated except to my wife. One thing I can partly tell now that he is dead. When he entered the CIA, he beat the polygraph test that all prospective agents have to take. (Always willing to take a risk.) He was determined to protect a family member from an embarrassing disclosure, and he did. I asked him how he accomplished that. "I guess that if you think you have a right to tell a lie, it will not register as one." At least it did not with him. He told me what he lied about, though I promised then to keep the secret, and I have.

From what I have said so far, it might be thought that Bill was self-centered. That was far from the case. He was thoughtful of others, almost to a fault. When he found that a summer intern at *National Review* was a promising young pianist who missed his practice hours back in the Midwest, he gave him the key to his town house (which had been UN secretary-general Dag Hammarskjöld's) and told him he could use it, while his wife was away, to play on his splendid Bösendorfer piano.

His generosity was unfailing. He liked to do things for people, surprising them with unexpected gifts. When the writer Wilfrid Sheed was ill, Bill, who knew he was a deep student of popular song, sent him the latest books on the subject. One day in the early sixties, a large package was brought to my front door. It was the twenty-four volumes of a new edition of the *Encyclopaedia Britannica*. Another time I got a package with framed copies of two charcoal portraits by the famous British newspaper artist David Low. These were studies of Gilbert Chesterton and Hilaire Belloc, and Bill knew I admired them. I asked where he had got the pictures. They were a gift to him from British broadcaster Alistair Cooke. Bill said, "They will mean more to you than to me."

He spent a lot of time thinking of what he could do for friends. When he heard that I needed a passport in a hurry, he pulled strings at the State Department to get it for me. On another occasion, when my newly wed Natalie and I could not find a cheap sea liner to England for our honeymoon, he found a ship for us leaving from Canada. Bill ingeniously invented a way to institutionalize his love for giving special gifts. Because his family was so prolific, he had forty-nine of what he called "N and Ns" (nieces and nephews). He took care of the education of many of these. But supplying necessities was not enough for him. He set up a fund he called the Dear Uncle Bill Trust (DUBT, soon pronounced "Doubt"), whose administrators gave surprise treats to N and Ns—a valuable guitar to an aspiring musician, a vacation in a favorite spot—on a rotating basis.

His desire to do things for people made him an inveterate matchmaker. He did all he could to encourage his Yale friend Brent Bozell to marry his favorite sister, Patricia (Trish). He hinted that another Yale undergraduate, Bill Coffin, should date another of his sisters. When I went to *National Review* in the summer of 1957, to talk about writing for him, I was just two months out of a Jesuit seminary, where I had been starved for opera music, and I soon found the Sam Goody music store. But I was staying in the Park Avenue apartment of Bill's father, which had no phonograph. When I mentioned this to Bill's young sister Maureen, who was working part-time at *National Review* that summer, she gave me the key to her apartment and said I could use the phonograph there any afternoon while she was at the office. Bill noticed that Maureen and I got along well, and when we would all go out to dinner at the end of the day, he put us together in one cab and took another with the rest of the party. We laughed at his matchmaking attempts. It was a family trait. Bill's sister Trish had met Pat Taylor in her freshman year at Vassar and decided Bill should marry her—as he did.

Perhaps it was his matchmaking urge that made Bill want to connect people with his church. When he learned as a child that any Christian can baptize a person in need of salvation, he and his sister Trish unobtrusively rubbed water on young visitors to their home while whispering the baptism formula.[1] In *National Review* circles, those who were not Catholics to begin with tended to enter the fold as converts: Brent Bozell, Russell Kirk, Willmoore Kendall, Frank Meyer, William Rusher, Jeffrey Hart, Joseph Sobran, Marvin Liebman, Robert Novak, Richard John Neuhaus. The major holdouts were James Burnham, a born Catholic who left the Church and never went back, and Whittaker Chambers, who was drawn to Richard Nixon's Quakerism. It was always easiest to be a Catholic around Bill, who became friendly with Malcolm Muggeridge when the British writer became a Catholic fellow traveler and Mother Teresa fan. I believe Bill was so nice to me in part because I am "incurably Catholic." There were different concentrations of people in the

National Review circle—Yale alumni, ex-Communists (Burnham, Meyer, Chambers, Willi Schlamm, Will Herburg, Freda Utley), ex–CIA members (Bill, his sister Priscilla, Burnham, Kendall)—but the Catholic contingent outnumbered all others.

Bill went to church on Sunday with the many Spanish-speaking house servants he had over the years. That did not fit his reputation as a snob. He was accused, at times, of being a social snob, an ideological snob, and an intellectual snob. None of these was the case in any but the most superficial sense.

Social Snob?

Bill could hardly have been a social snob when he was playing matchmaker for his sister and me. I was a penniless nobody. For that matter, Brent Bozell had no significant money or social standing when (with Bill's encouragement) he married Bill's sister Trish. Brent had gone to Yale on a double scholarship, from the GI Bill and from an American Legion oratory award. Where his family was concerned, Bill always cared more about a person's being Catholic and conservative than about his or her being rich. I passed the Catholic test, and came close enough on the conservative point, in 1957, for him to hint that Maureen and I might be made for each other.

Despite his religious and ideological preferences, Bill was basically egalitarian. Though he always used proper titles for guests on his TV show, he was "Bill" to everyone from the moment one met him. He treated all ranks at the magazine with equal dignity, and all called him Bill. When confusion arose because Bill Rusher was in the magazine's office as its publisher, younger people on the staff referred to Big Bill (Buckley) and Little Bill (Rusher) when a distinction had to be made. Needless to say, Little Bill was not fond of the nickname.

There was never any "side" to Bill. In this he was unlike his wife. He always dressed like a rumpled undergraduate, while she had Bill Blass and other designers dancing attendance on her. Bill and Pat were deeply in love—each called the other "Ducky," as Spencer Tracy's and Katharine Hepburn's characters call each other "Pinky" in the movie *Adam's Rib*. But the Tracy and Hepburn characters had their differences, and so did the Buckleys. They had different (though overlapping) social circles. Bill was amused by her friends (including Truman Capote), and he dutifully went to some of her charity events, where he was often bored. She dutifully went on his short sailing jaunts, but some of his intellectual friends—like the literary critic Hugh Kenner—she treated as a nuisance.

Pat had left Vassar after only two years, and her son wrote: "Her cap-and-gownless departure from Poughkeepsie left her, for the rest of her life, with a deep-seated insecurity that manifested itself aggressively, especially after the supernumerary glass of wine. . . . Pup remarked to me after she died that he had not once, in fifty-seven years of marriage, seen her read a nonfiction book"—an exaggeration, no doubt, but a telling one.[2] Since Bill was often away on lecture tours or sailing trips or foreign interviews, Pat was often escorted to fashionable events, like other socialites with busy husbands, by the gay men known as "walkers"—the type Woody Harrelson played in Paul Schrader's movie *The Walker* (2007). Her son, Christopher, notes some of Pat's many walkers: Jerry Zipkin, Christopher Hewett, Bill Blass, Peter Glenville, Valentino, John Richardson, Truman Capote, "and others." [3]

Bill's style was rather plainer, though he was ridiculed for describing in great detail the limousine he had specially redesigned as a kind of traveling office. He was accused of snobbishly showing off his fancy car. But he had only realized the advantage of having a chauffeur when he ran for mayor of New York in 1965. Then he needed a car to get him to events when there was no time or place for parking it himself. He saw that he could do his endless dictating of letters and columns on the move, and he kept the Irish Catholic driver who had seen him through the campaign. Before that race, he regularly rode around New York on his motorbike. And he was driving his own (modest) car when I met him in 1957. After I arrived from Michigan at his office in New York, where he had asked me to come talk about writing for *National Review*, he asked where I had left my suitcase. I said, "At the airport." I thought I might be heading right back to Michigan at the end of that day.

He told me to wait while he finished his editing, then drove me to LaGuardia. After I picked up my bag, he drove us out to his home in Stamford, Connecticut, where we talked, swam, and ate dinner. Then he drove me back into New York, put me up in his father's apartment at 80 Park Avenue, and turned around to drive back to Stamford. He was my chauffeur that day. It was the kind of thoughtfulness many people experienced from him.

Ideological Snob?

There was a better case for thinking Bill had ideological prejudices. But when he established *National Review,* he observed no
ideological test for all those he hired or tried to hire. He wanted
good writing and intellectual stimulation. That is why he
printed non-right-wingers like Murray Kempton, John Leonard,
Joan Didion, Renata Adler, and Arlene Croce. Later, he sailed or
skied with John Kenneth Galbraith and Walter Cronkite (I sailed
with both), not because they were celebrities but because he
liked them and admired their minds.

The real measure of Bill was the extent to which he overcame the prejudices he began with because of his family. His
delightful mother was a southern belle from New Orleans
whose grandfather had been a Confederate officer at Shiloh.
She had the attitude toward blacks of her upbringing. One
time, when we were sailing and stopped at Charleston, South
Carolina, Bill took me to his father's winter home. When we
arrived, we were greeted by a black retainer who had known
Bill from his childhood—he called him "Master Billy." It was
not surprising that Bill and I would initially disagree about
the civil rights movement. In a notorious 1957 editorial called
"Why the South Must Prevail," Bill defended segregation because whites were "the advanced race," and "the claims of
civilization superseded those of universal suffrage."[4] We argued over this, and his biographer says that my views gradu-
ally had some effect: "Under the influence of conservative
proponents of civil rights like Wills and the heated debate

about civil rights taking place in the country, Buckley began to distinguish *National Review*'s and the conservative positions from that of Southern racists."[5]

Another burden from Bill's early days was his father's anti-Semitism, a harder thing for him to conquer, since he honored his father so profoundly. A close friend of Bill's on the *Yale Daily News* was Tom Guinzberg, later the publisher of Viking Press. Guinzberg and Bill's sister Jane were on the verge of being engaged, and Bill's father said that Bill, using his friendship with Guinzberg, should prevent a Jew from joining the family. To his later regret, he intervened without telling his sister. For once, he was a match breaker rather than a matchmaker. I was with him the night he finally confessed to Jane what he had done behind her back. She said it did not matter—the marriage would not have worked. Bill said, "I wish I had known that earlier—I have been reproaching myself all these years." Bill not only broke *National Review* away from right-wing journals that harbored anti-Semites. When he found that a book reviewer (Revilo Oliver) or one of his editors (M. Joseph Sobran) was writing anti-Semitic stuff in other venues, he banned those writers' further appearance in the magazine. Bill had become so sensitive to the problem that he wrote a book on the anti-Semitic tendencies of right-wingers like Sobran and Patrick Buchanan.[6]

By the time of his death, even Bill's earlier critics admitted that he had done much to make conservatism respectable by purging it of racist and fanatical traits earlier embedded in the movement. He distanced his followers from the southern prejudices of George Wallace, the anti-Semitism of the Liberty Lobby, the fanaticism of the John Birch Society, the glorification of selfishness by Ayn Rand (famously excoriated in *National Review* by Whittaker Chambers), the paranoia and conspiratorialism of the neocons. In each of these cases, some right-wingers tried to cut off donations to *National Review*, but Bill stood his ground. In doing so, he elevated the discourse of American politics, making civil debate possible between responsible liberals and conservatives.

Intellectual Snob?

Bill was considered an elitist because he loved to use big words. This was a part of his playfulness. He liked to play games in general, and word games were especially appealing to him. He did it not from hauteur but from impishness. He used the big words for their own sake, even when he was not secure in their meaning. One of his most famous usages poisoned the general currency, especially among young conservatives trying to imitate him. They took "oxymoron" in the sense he gave it, though that was the opposite of its true meaning. He thought it was a fancier word for "contradiction" (a perfectly good word that needs no fancy dress), so young imitators would say that an intelligent liberal is an oxymoron. But the Greek word means something that is surprisingly *true*, a paradox, a "shrewd dumbness."

Bill's love of exotic locutions came out when he asked me, one time, for the meaning of a word I had written, "subumbrous." I said it meant cloaked in darkness. He protested that he could not find the word in any of his dictionaries. No wonder, I said; I made it up from the Latin *sub umbra*. He loved that—it continued the word games. But his lunge toward risky words was like his other ventures into risk. I wrote him once giving him five examples of Latin words he had used in the wrong cases. He did not yield easily. He said he used not the grammatically correct forms but the ones he thought would be most familiar to his audience. It was one of the few times I saw him resort to a populist argument.

Bill was not, and did not pretend to be, a real intellectual. He gave up the "big book" that his father and others were urging him to write. For years he tried to do a continuation of José Ortega y Gasset's *Revolt of the Masses*. This had been a sacred text for his father's guru, Albert Jay Nock. Bill took intellectual comrades like Hugh Kenner with him for his winter break in Switzerland, to help him get a grip on this ambitious project. But he told me he realized in time that this was not his métier. He was not a reflective thinker. He was a quick responder. He wrote rapidly because he was quickly bored. His gifts were facility, flash, and charm, not depth or prolonged wrestling with a problem. He made it his vocation to be the promoter, popularizer, and moderator of the conservative movement, defending it from liberal critics with wit and effrontery. In this he was entirely successful.

Bill needed people around him all the time. Frequently, when he told me he had to write a column, I would offer to withdraw from the boat cabin or hotel room or office where we were. He urged me not to, and as he typed (with great speed and accuracy) he would keep on talking off and on, reading a sentence to me, trying out a word, saying that something he was saying would annoy old So-and-So. When I appeared on his TV show to discuss a new book of mine, it was clear to me that he had not read the book—he was given notes on each author he interviewed. Once he asked me if I had read all of Adam Smith's *Wealth of Nations*. I said yes. "Haven't you?" He had not. *"Das Kapital?"* No, he had not read that through either. I suspect the same was true of capitalist classics he referred to—by Ludwig von Mises, Wilhelm Röpke, and others. He could defend them with great panache. But he did not want to sit all by himself for a long time reading them. One of his teachers at Yale, the philosopher Paul Weiss, told me that Bill was very good at discussing books he had not read. His garage-office in Stamford was piled high with mounds of books, mostly sent to him, hundreds of them, in no order. That is not how a person who loves books keeps them.

Bill was heatedly attacked by Catholic liberals when he dismissed papal criticism of capitalism. He objected to John XXIII's encyclical *Mater et Magistra* (the Church as "Mother and Teacher") for its challenge to the free market. I joked that his attitude was *"Mater sí, Magistra no,"* playing on a slogan of the time, *"Cuba sí, Castro no."* He printed the quip in the magazine and was attacked on the assumption that the saying was his own and he was rejecting the whole teaching role of the Church. He questioned me about Church teachings. He felt insecure because his Catholic education was so exiguous—it amounted to one year at a Jesuit prep school in England. I had been entirely educated in Catholic schools before entering graduate school at Yale, and he exaggerated what knowledge that had given me.

He wanted to know more about encyclicals. I told him I did not know much. I had read carefully the so-called social encyclicals—*Rerum Novarum* (1891) and *Quadragesimo Anno* (1931)—because Chesterton admired their praise of medieval guilds. He asked if I would bone up on the subject, and I agreed to. (Once again, he did not want to read all those boring encyclicals himself.) After I had done some research on the matter, he drove up from Stamford to New Haven to spend an afternoon discussing the subject. He had been challenged to a debate with an editor of *Commonweal*, William Clancy. Bill suggested that each side be defended by a two-man team—by Bill and me on one side, by Clancy and a partner of his choosing on the other. Clancy turned down the idea. Nonetheless, when it came time for the debate, to be held across the river from Manhattan in New Jersey, Bill asked me to go along with him for some last-minute preparation in the car. Once again, he was driving his own car. We had to grab a quick dinner before the event, so we stopped at a greasy spoon in New Jersey. When Bill asked for a bottle of red wine, it came out ice-cold, so he asked that it be run under hot water for a while, and we kept up our informal seminar on encyclicals.

Bill handled the debate with his customary forensic stylishness. But the Catholic attacks on him continued. They had become so voluminous at this point that our friend Neil McCaffrey made a collection of them, to be published with Neil's sulfurous comments on each item. Bill asked me to write an introduction to the collection, on the status of encyclicals. When Neil had the book ready, Bill asked me to come down from New Haven to his garage at Stamford. He found Neil's intemperate running commentary embarrassing. He wanted to cancel the project—unless I was willing to expand my introduction, incorporating some of the attacks into a calmer treatment of the matter. I said that I doubted Neil would be amenable to having his concept taken away from him. Bill said I should just leave that to him. Somehow, with his smooth persuasiveness, he took the project over without losing Neil's friendship, and I published *Politics and Catholic Freedom*, the first of my books on the papacy.

Bill lived and wrote and lectured—and played and socialized and exercised—at a furious pace. Partly this was because he bored so easily. But partly it was to make money. He was commonly thought of as a spoiled rich boy. But he had never had the kind of money people imagined. His wife did—she came from a far wealthier family than his. But he did not want to live on her inheritance. Bill's oilman father had drilled many a dry hole. Bill's biographer did the numbers, and concluded that the senior Buckley's money was exaggerated.[7] After the father's death, Bill's oldest brother, John, a heavy drinker, did not run the oil company with great skill.

Bill's own investments, especially in radio stations, rather set back than advanced his financial affairs—as always, he was too in love with risk. Bill made a good living, initially from his heavy lecture schedule, then from his widely syndicated newspaper column, then from his profitable series of spy novels. But he worked for much of his own money. I remember how delighted he was, in 1960, when for the first time he was paid a dollar a word for a magazine article (a good sum then). He did not, of course, have to work for a living. He could have lived on a lower scale than the one he maintained. But he wanted to support the swashbuckling yachts, the custom-made limousine, the ski lodge in Switzerland, and the great generosity of his gifts to others; and he did not want to do this on his wife's money. Thus he secretly acquired what some will consider his least plausible identity, that of a working stiff.

For a longer time than I now wish, Bill and I were estranged. For the first twelve years after we met, we were in almost constant contact. I sailed with him often (crewing for two of his international ocean races). We traveled together—in Ireland, to observe the Catholic-Protestant conflict, we went to an Ian Paisley sermon and a Bernadette Devlin rally. We attended two national political conventions. While working on his biography, I talked to him almost every day. We conferred on Catholic matters (especially during the Second Vatican Council). But the convulsions of the sixties and their aftermath tore many people apart, and they did that with us. He was a hard supporter of the Vietnam War, though I went to jail twice to protest it. I called his dear friend Henry Kissinger a war criminal (for approving the use of flechette bombs in cities). Though Bill had abondoned the southern view of black inferiority, he thought that Martin Luther King Jr. was hurting America in its struggle with Communism by criticizing its racism. Even my own friend at the magazine, Frank Meyer, tried to have my comments against Richard Nixon killed. My critical review of Whittaker Chambers's book of essays was spiked (I published it in *Modern Age*). The final break came when Bill refused to publish an essay in which I argued that there was no conservative rationale for our ruinous engagement in Vietnam. For the next thirty years communication between us was at first minimal, and then nonexistent.

When I moved out of my office at Northwestern, reducing

my library to what would fit into my home, I gave a used-book store owner the pick of my volumes at the university. He went off with many titles that Bill had inscribed to me, and when some of Bill's irate fans found them in the store, they bought them and sent them back to him, calling me an ingrate for selling his gifts. When Bill's service in the CIA under Howard Hunt came to light during the Watergate scandal, I wrote a column about Bill's CIA connections. Perhaps he thought I was using confidential knowledge he had given me on the tapes I made for his biography; but I used nothing that was not public knowledge by then. He circulated my column to the *National Review* board of editors with his marginal notation, "I think we should smash him"—an item that his biographer found in his papers at Yale.[8] For a time the magazine ran a recurring feature, "The Wills Watch," recording the latest liberal abomination I was guilty of. The principal Wills Watcher was M. Joseph Sobran. A man who later became an editor at the magazine, Rick Brookhiser, wrote:

> It was clear to me as a reader of *National Review* that Wills had been an important figure at the magazine, if only because the magazine continued to needle him. One cover pasted Wills's head on a famous image of Black Panther Huey Newton, enthroned with spear and shotgun on his wicker chair.[9]

John Leonard, another "*National Review* apostate," as Bill called us, told his biographer: "When Garry said what was happening to blacks was more important than what was reflected in the magazine, and it hurts me personally, he spoke to the best part, that most vulnerable part, of the Buckleys. It [the disagreement] went from blacks to Nixon to Vietnam." [10] Sobran, comparing me with another "defector," said: "I don't think Kevin Phillips got anywhere near his heart the way that Garry Wills had. He didn't covet Phillips's esteem the way he had Garry's." [11]

When Bill went to speak at Yale, on one of his innumerable visits there, my son, Garry L. Wills, was in the host line of students receiving him to shake hands. When my son gave his name as Garry Wills, Bill said, "No relation, I hope." Garry, who can be as pixieish as Bill, serenely said, "None at all"—which left Bill turning back with puzzled looks as he moved on down the line. On another occasion, Bill's son, Christopher, whom I had met years before as a boat boy on Bill's yacht, and who was now a student at Yale, invited me to come speak at the annual *Yale Daily News* dinner. I suspected that Christopher was in one of his moments of conflict with his father, and I declined to take part in that drama.

But Bill's wonderful and selfless sister Priscilla, who always kept me in her loving circle, trusted to the real regard Bill and I still had for each other. She called me in 2005 to say it was silly for two people who had been such friends not to be talking to each other. She set up a dinner at our old restaurant, Paone, where Bill and I resumed our friendship and, after that, our correspondence. Bill wrote to tell me he had given my *What Jesus Meant* as a Christmas gift to friends. It was clear that our disagreements had been transcended. Bill even ended up a critic of the Iraq War—unlike the Vietnam War he had once defended, leading us to part company so many years before. When Bill suggested on *Charlie Rose* that he was ready to die, I found his words heartbreaking, and I wrote to tell him so. When Priscilla told me that in his last days, weakened by emphysema, he could not move across the room without her pulling him up and supporting him, I thought of the figure—lithe, athletic, prompt— who brought his sailboat to rest with one deft turn of his foot on the wheel, and I grieved for one who brought so much excitement into my life.

NOTES

1. William F. Buckley Jr., *Nearer, My God: An Autobiography of Faith* (Harcourt Brace & Company, 1997), pp. 9–10.

2. Christopher Buckley, *Losing Mum and Pup* (Twelve, 2009), pp. 57–58.

3. Ibid., pp. 65–67.

4. John B. Judis, *William F. Buckley, Jr., Patron Saint of the Conservatives* (Simon & Schuster, 1988), p. 128.

5. Ibid., p. 191.

6. William F. Buckley Jr., *In Search of Anti-Semitism* (Continuum, 1992).

7. Judis, op. cit., p. 164.

8. Ibid., p. 359.

9. Richard Brookhiser, *Right Time, Right Place: Coming of Age with William F. Buckley Jr. and the Conservative Movement* (Basic Books, 2009), p. 32.

10. Judis, op. cit., p. 325.

11. Ibid., pp. 379–80.

14

Natalie

Though Bill did not succeed in matching me with his sister Maureen, he inadvertently proved a matchmaker after all. He sent me where I met Natalie. When I arrived at *National Review*'s office in 1957, invited there because of an article I had sent "over the transom" about *Time* magazine, I told Bill I was doing my graduate-school work in Greek tragedy, and he offered me a job as the magazine's theater critic. I turned him down—I meant to return to classes at the end of the summer. He had called me up at Xavier University in Cincinnati, where I was serving as an assistant to a patristics scholar, collating Chrysostom manuscripts. I had left the seminary so suddenly that I had no time to apply to graduate schools—my seminary Greek teacher had hastily arranged for me to attend Xavier, a Jesuit school, while applying to other graduate programs.

Bill, as usual, tried to help me in my quest for a scholarship. He invited the classics scholar Revilo Oliver to come with us for a day sail, and asked Revilo if he could offer me financial support at the University of Illinois. Revilo said he would be glad to. "We can give you a first-rate education, but you will not have the first-rate chances at a good position you would get by coming from an Ivy League school." He recommended that I apply to them, and if I could not get a scholarship that would support me there, then he would take me on at Illinois. Luckily, I got a McCormick Fellowship at Yale.

When I said I could not accept Bill's offer of regular employment, he asked if I would stay for the rest of that summer, living in his father's suite at 80 Park Avenue (since the senior Buckley was out of town), and doing odd jobs for the magazine. I reviewed the plays that were still running that summer: *Auntie Mame* with Rosalind Russell, *New Girl in Town* with Gwen Verdon, *Long Day's Journey into Night* with Jason Robards. I wrote about books for Frank Meyer, the literary editor. Then Bill had the typically wild idea of sending me briefly down to Washington to write about the Senate hearings into Jimmy Hoffa's mob connections. I said that I knew nothing about labor unions. Bill swept my objections aside. "Go see Suzie, she knows all about unions. Then I'll call Murray Kempton and ask him to give you some information."

Suzie was Suzanne La Follette, the feminist and libertarian who had edited the *Freeman* with Bill's hero Albert Jay Nock. A vinous lunch with her taught me little, so I went over to Kempton's office at the *New York Post*. He was working on his column when I arrived, but after Bill had called him he had laid out all his newspaper clip files on Hoffa. He told me to browse through them and we could talk later on. When he finished his column, he invited me to take the train with him to stay the night at his home in Princeton, where he could cook me dinner (his wife was away for the week). After listening to his favorite recording of *Don Giovanni*, we talked (and drank) late into the night. Among other things, he said he always had trouble criticizing

Hoffa because he was the only labor leader he knew who was faithful to his wife.

The next morning we overslept and ran for the train. We were running for it as it started to move. Younger and nimbler, I jumped on board, only to learn it was the wrong train, one that was being shunted to a siding. Murray had to have the station-master pull it back. This gave me just enough time to catch a plane for Washington. Sam Jones, the first Washington editor for *National Review*, gave me lunch at the Press Club, caught me up on the state of the Senate hearing, and got me into the press gallery, where I watched the Kennedy brothers grill Hoffa—John as a committee member, Robert as the staff investigator. Robert said Hoffa had the opportunity to be a great benefit or a great burden for society. Hoffa said he would try to live up to both responsibilities. The hearings were unexpectedly suspended at the end of the afternoon. I called Bill and asked what I should do. He told me to fly back to New York and take the train for Stamford, since he was throwing a party for the magazine's editors.

On the Eastern Airlines plane, a flight attendant (then called stewardess) offered to hang up my heavy suit jacket—I had only one suit, the winter weight the seminary gives to any person who leaves. I said it had my pens and notes, and hung on to it. The flight's landing was delayed for a long time as we were stacked up over LaGuardia. There was an empty seat beside me. The stewardess sat down and told me I was too young to be reading Bergson. She had read (as had I) Walter Kaufmann's description of Bergson in *Existentialism*. Later, when we met Kaufmann in Acapulco at a Young Presidents' Organization

conference, we told him he had been our Galahalt. The stewardess had a pretty Italian face of the *mandorla* (almond-shaped)
sort Modigliani liked to paint. And mischievous chocolate
eyes.

We shared, as it turned out in our talk, things other than an
interest in Walter Kaufmann—especially a love of opera. Since
our landing was so delayed, I told her I was missing a party in
Connecticut. Where? she asked. Stamford. "I drive by there on
my way home to Wallingford—I'll drop you off." She told me
where to wait while she checked in and picked up her car. She
said the car was a convertible blue Alfa Romeo Spider, a thing I
had never heard of. On the drive to Stamford, we had more talk.
She was a Catholic and we differed on some Church teachings.
She was Italian-American, and we talked of Italian art. She had
been a sociology major at Sweet Briar (which is why she read
Kaufmann), and I told her about my seminary studies. Her
mother owned a bridal shop, and she knew clothes. She said she
had wondered at my blue serge suit in summer when she asked
for the jacket.

I thought she would come into the party, and our talk had
continued to the arrival at Bill's house. She said she was still in
her stewardess uniform and did not want to go in. From my
recent-seminary ineptness, I let her drive off without getting
her phone number. When she got home and told Lydia, her
mother, that she had met an interesting guy on the plane, Lydia
asked if she would see him again. No, Natalie said, and Lydia
went "*Ha*-ha."

At the end of Bill's party, one of the editors drove me back to
80 Park. In the morning I called Eastern Airlines and said I

wanted the phone number for a stewardess called Natalie, with an Italian last name beginning C (I had already forgotten her family name, Cavallo, though we had joked about its meaning "horse"). I reported that she had been on flight number (whatever it was) from Washington, as if that would give me the key to her identity. I was too naive to realize that airlines do not give out such information. I was informed of official policy, emphatically. Despite this hard rebuff the first time, I got up nerve to call back and say that I had left in her car a marked-up advance copy of a book I was reviewing, which I had to get back immediately. "Don't give me her number," I said. "Give her mine, and tell her to call me only if she finds the book in her car." She got a sardonic morning call: "Did you give some guy a ride last night?" I did not realize what trouble I could have got her into.

She went out to the Alfa, searched it thoroughly, found there was no book, smiled, and dialed my number. "Did you really leave a book in my car?" she asked. "No." "Then why did you say you did?" "Because I want to see you again." "When?" "How about today?" She went to her mother's shop, got a new dress, told her "*Ha*-ha," and caught the train for Manhattan. I said on the phone I would wait for her at the clock desk in the middle of Grand Central Station (one of the iconic spots of our history). We went to the big 1957 Picasso exhibit at the Museum of Modern Art, and I put her up at a hotel around the corner from 80 Park so we could spend the rest of the weekend together. Throughout that summer she was with me whenever she was not flying.

She told me she could not figure me out at first—I was

•

clearly a rube from the Midwest, newly arrived in New York with only one out-of-season suit to my name, yet I was living in a luxurious Park Avenue suite. The suite was so large that it had an entire wing I had not discovered till I went into the kitchen one morning and found a beautiful young woman there—she was the wife of Reid Buckley, Bill's brother. She and Reid had come in while I slept, and settled for a brief stay in the other wing of the suite. Natalie said she wondered why I knew and took her to some "in" restaurants of the time (Mercurio, Charles à la Pomme Souffle, Paone, the Black Angus)— they were all places where Bill had taken me. She thought it odd I rode cabs everywhere and never the subway—I did not yet know how to take the subway. I had tickets to the best plays in town. I explained, step by step, how I knew these things, and said she must meet Bill.

She did meet him, in the best of circumstances—on a day sail in his boat. (Sailing with Bill was one of life's great experiences.) She was charmed by Bill, of course. But after we left the boat, she said, "Be careful." Why? "He's dangerous." Why? "He absorbs people." I knew then what a wise person I was dealing with in Natalie. Her quick judgment was confirmed, over and over, as I got to know Bill and his effect on others, his matchmaking, his religious proselytizing, his favors done and lives arranged. When I was writing my book on Bill, I met with the woman who had been the Buckley family's music teacher in his childhood, Marjorie Gifford. Though she was a young performer and scholar in her twenties when she went to the Buckley home in Sharon, commissioned to teach all the younger children, Bill and his siblings called her "Old Lady" and grew very fond of her. Bill was her best pupil (though she said he never got the harmonies straight).

I had arranged to meet Old Lady at Bill's Stamford home when he and his wife were in Manhattan. She sat at Bill's piano as she remembered the years she spent with the Buckley family. It was the happiest time of her life, in one way, and the most destructive. I asked why. She said she gave up her own musical ambitions and began living entirely wrapped up in the Buckley family's fun and games. She developed a young girl's crush on Bill's father and lost much of her own future life. She told me what this did to her was not the family's fault. "They could not help it that they were so charming."

When I gave up the idea of writing Bill's biography, he turned the project over to a young man who had done the cover story about him for *Time* magazine. Bill asked me to give him the tapes I had recorded. I withheld and destroyed some of the most intimate, including Old Lady's—I felt that she had been so open with me that I would not trust her memories to another. Let the new scribe elicit them if she cared to tell another person of her sorrow.

Hers was a tale I heard or observed in various registers over the years. Once, when I visited Willmoore Kendall, Bill's teacher at Yale who was teaching then at Dallas University, he claimed that Brent Bozell, his other Yale student, would have been a fine and productive senator from Nebraska if he had not been sucked into the Buckley family in Connecticut. Brent first became dependent on the Buckleys, then rebellious against them, then more Catholic than Bill in a fierce rejection of America's separation of church and state. "Buckleys," Willmoore said, "swallow people." I suppose I would have been swallowed if Maureen and I had married, as Bill was prompting us.

I continued to see Natalie after our summer in New York ended. I had to finish my bridge year at Xavier before accepting the next year's fellowship at Yale. I got back to New York on weekends when I could afford to. She "deadheaded" free flights to the town nearest Cincinnati where Eastern Airlines flew—Louisville, as it turned out, where we stayed at my Irish grandmother's house. The first time Natalie came in at the Louisville airport, it was late at night. She called my grandmother's number and a woman answered. When Natalie asked for me, the woman made an angry response—"Decent ladies do not call on men at night"—and slammed the phone down. Natalie had no other way to reach me but that number, so she had to try it again (as I'd had to call Eastern Airlines again when I got rebuffed). Fortunately, this time I got to the phone first. "What was *that*?" she asked. "Oh, that was just Cornelia. I forgot to tell you about her." Cornelia was my epileptic aunt, whose brain was affected by seizures when she was growing up, before modern drugs and treatments for epilepsy could have helped her. Cornelia's mental age was about twelve, and my sister and I had loved her as a playmate in our childhood.

It was a lot easier to see Natalie when I went to Yale. New Haven was just thirteen miles from her home in Wallingford. In a battered old car my father had given me, I made record time back and forth to her house, where I watched football games on TV with her father and got to know and love the extended network of Italian families that filled her neighborhood, where the men played boccie in the street on Sundays and grew grapes in their backyard and made homemade wine. Natalie quit flying and took a job in New Haven so we could have more time together. We talked about marrying, but I had little money beyond my fellowship, which was barely supporting me through graduate school. She said she could work, and she would sell her Alfa. I was making something extra by writing children's Bible pamphlets for Neil McCaffrey at Doubleday. But it did not seem enough.

One night we went to Yale's law school to hear a talk by the controversial congressman Adam Clayton Powell, who did not show up. As we were walking back to my room in the Hall of Graduate Studies, she stopped on the sidewalk by the New Haven cemetery and started stamping her foot with Italian fieriness: "We're *never* getting married." The spot is a revered one for me. I said let's go to my room and call our parents with the news that we are getting married. Years later I was on Tavis Smiley's TV show, and I found that he has a practice, after the broadcast ends, of asking his guest of the day what is the best advice he or she ever received. When I said my best advice was Natalie's telling me we *had* to get married (not the best way of putting it), he collapsed with laughter.

Bill Buckley, Frank Meyer, and Neil McCaffrey were ushers at our wedding, and we left immediately after for England. I would spend our honeymoon studying the papers of G. K. Chesterton. We had a letter of introduction from my friend Wilfrid Sheed to his mother, Maisie Ward, Chesterton's first biographer. We went to the London headquarters of her publishing house, Sheed and Ward, and she came out of her office to a waiting room, carrying a big book of glossy photos. As part of her do-good activities, she found cheap lodgings for penurious young couples. She thought that was what we had come for. Actually, we wanted her to intervene with Chesterton's executor, the keeper of his papers, his former secretary Dorothy Collins. Ms. Collins had first answered my letter asking to see the papers with a kind permission, but then had followed up with a letter saying she could not allow it. We seemed to have made the expensive trip for nothing. But with the help of Maisie Ward, the first permission was reinstated, and we went off to Beaconsfield, to Chesterton's house (a converted theater) that Ms. Collins had inherited.

She greeted us at the door and said that she and her woman companion were just tuning in to their favorite show on the telly; would we sit and watch with them? It was *I Love Lucy* (a show I could never stand, for all its frenetic screaming). After the show was over, she served an elaborate English tea. After that, I asked about looking into the papers. She said they were up in the attic. She pointed the way for me while Natalie stayed behind to talk with the ladies. (Though I am terrible at small talk with strangers, Natalie can find things to speak about with anyone, which has rescued me in many situations.) Up in the attic, I saw why her friends had advised Ms. Collins against letting more people look at the papers. They were strewn about, in trunks, on tables, on the floor, not kept in any order. I would learn that others had marked them up, taken them off, treated them with no regard—even though the collection contained letters from T. S. Eliot, G. B. Shaw, H. G. Wells, and others, as well as many drawings and sketches by Chesterton himself (who started out as an art student at the Slade School).

I tried to separate out the anguished drawings and poems he had written in his depressed adolescence—the object of my first enquiry. Then I went downstairs and asked how I could study the papers without disturbing Ms. Collins in her home. She answered that she had a big suitcase I could fill with what I wanted and take to London for leisurely perusal. When I finished with one load of the papers, I could bring them back and get more. No wonder she had been taken advantage of.

Back in our London flat, I sorted out the things I wanted to have copies of (this was before Xerox), and Natalie typed them for me. I had asked her to learn typing before we married, and she promised that she would do so for this trip and then would never use the skill again—a promise she kept. Her typing, unlike mine, was immaculate, indeed flawless, and she regretted, years later when she got her first computer, that she had not kept up her practice.

At the end of my trips back and forth to Beaconsfield, I asked Ms. Collins if I could buy one of the Chesterton drawings from the attic. She had told me how Hilaire Belloc, wanting to sell a novel to his publisher, would come to Beaconsfield and describe the plot, while Chesterton deftly illustrated the story in a series of pencil sketches. There were often more drawings than the publisher could use, and these would be returned to Chesterton. I had spotted an unused one from Belloc's *The Postmaster General*. When I asked to buy it, Dorothy gave it to me. It now hangs in our house next to the David Low portrait of Chesterton that Bill gave me.

When I was not working in London on the papers from

Beaconsfield, or in the Chesterton collections at the British Museum, Natalie and I had a great summer in that heyday of British theater. England was still suffering from World War II—the swinging sixties of Mary Quant and the Beatles had not yet arrived—and tickets for plays were as cheap as those for movies. We had so little money that Natalie, who hated the English food of that day, lived for long stretches on anchovy sandwiches from the Italian delis near our flat. We proved that summer that a famous book of the time, *Europe on Five Dollars a Day*, could be vindicated. Toward the end of the summer, Natalie had a near miscarriage from her pregnancy with our first child (we had celebrated the news of him with our sole London splurge on the famous prime ribs at Simpson's). The doctor ordered her to go to bed and remain immobile for a while. I found an old four-foot-tall floor radio in a used-goods store and staggered back carrying it for her to listen to. There was no air-conditioning in the flat, so we could hear Italian neighbors playing opera records in the building across the street. One Sunday when they put on an aria by Beniamino Gigli, I went across and asked them to play it again, louder.

Though she was now in bed, we continued to work on the Chesterton papers together, establishing an intellectual partnership that would continue through the next half century. Everything I wrote in the coming years she went over, for accuracy, clarity, repetitions, and tact. I had many occasions to be grateful for her interventions—as when I wrote some sharp things about Richard Nixon's wife, Pat, and she rightly insisted that I remove them. For years I wrote everything in longhand, and had to read the copy to her, since my handwriting is so awful she could not decipher it. After I started using a computer, she read from the printouts of the first draft.

She not only collaborated with the writing. She has been diplomat and intermediary on our many travels. In Scotland, I could not understand the Glaswegian accent of a worker for us, but she had the ear for it. In Italy, though I read the newspapers to her in the morning, since she has forgotten the Italian she learned as a child before speaking English, her ear for the language of her relatives is still good enough to catch the spoken Italian word that I miss. In Israel, her Mediterranean looks make people talk to her when my Irish face looks unpromising.

Only in Greece and Japan did the language barrier baffle us. In Athens, when she left me studying grave sites in the cemetery (Kerameikos) to walk back to our hotel, she was pelted by women with olive pits as an intruder in their neighborhood, and had no words to respond. In Japan, when we took a trip without the interpreter that the Japan Society had given us, an earthquake made the trains all shut down automatically, so that the schedules were scrambled. We were in a provincial city where few spoke English (and that un-understandable) and we could not read the newly posted times—we had to stand by each train as it came in, gesturing like Clark Gable trying to hitchhike in *It Happened One Night,* saying "Tokyo?"

On the other hand, her gift for talking to anyone about anything struck me with new respect when we were given a concert of private recordings by the Japanese composer Toru Takemitsu, including one he had written on a visit to America, his *Long Island Suite.* Natalie went over to him after the performance and said, "I love your suite." He answered, "I'm so glad," gesturing down to his lapels. "I designed it myself." Natalie did not miss a beat. She said, "Oh, do you design all your clothes?"

As our children went off to college, Natalie added another to her many gifts by taking up photography. She got press credentials to the political conventions I attended, and her shots from the floor and from peripheral events gave me new material to write about. Her pictures in Venice became illustrations for the book I wrote about that city (and for its cover, designed by our son). We collaborated on a syndicated newspaper series about Israel, my words, her pictures. One day, when she was shooting scenes in Jerusalem's Old City on the Sabbath, some Orthodox young men in black hats and side-curls came at her menacingly, determined to take the camera away from her. I, who had retired from the heat to sit in a shady arcade, came running over to her, and they beat a hasty retreat. It reminded me of a time in Milan when we were walking to the Castello and young boys approached her crying that birds had shat on the back of her coat—in fact the boys had thrown some slime there as an excuse to get near enough to grab her impressive-looking camera. Again, I was in the background, but I came up yelling *"Ladri,"* and they scurried off.

I rescued her less often than she did me. When I was in a car accident in Texas, she told the doctors on the telephone to have a cosmetic surgeon present to stitch up my face. Then she called on our daughter in New York, who knows about medical facilities, and the two of them flew down to have me transferred from the first hospital at hand (which had been ineffectual) to a famous one in Houston. The two made a great defensive team. Natalie had done the same kind of thing when our daughter almost lost an eye to a dog bite. Natalie told the doctors, who cared only about saving the eye, that she wanted that as much as they did, but she also wanted a cosmetic surgeon to be there, considering the long-term appearance of Lydia's face. After hours of surgery on our daughter, when the doctors came out and said they had indeed saved the eye, I was the one who flopped over to a chair to avoid fainting, while my strong wife upheld the family honor.

I could go on forever—about Natalie's Italian cooking (her soups and pastas), her garden, her remodelings of our home and the art she acquired for it. But she orders me not to do this, and she is she who must be obeyed. Think, nonetheless, of my quandary. I can scare myself silly by considering the close calls in my life. What if Bill had not sent me to the Hoffa hearing in Washington? What if I had not caught that particular Eastern flight back? What if she had not been assigned to the plane that day? What if the seat next to me had not been empty? What if we had not been delayed above LaGuardia for so long? What if I had not been reading Bergson? What if either of us had not read Walter Kaufmann? What if Bill's party had been in his Manhattan house instead of Stamford? What if the airline had not called her with my phony book story? What if she had believed it when I said she should call only if she found the non-existent book?

The odds were against me all along the way. Despite this, I won, and we celebrated our fiftieth wedding anniversary last year. I'm dazed each time I remember that she tried to take my jacket, sat down beside me, warned me against Bill, stamped on the sidewalk, went with me to England, shared my love of opera, corrected my books, bore me three beautiful children, and made my life endlessly rich with meaning. Inside our wedding rings are inscriptions from the marriage poems of Catullus. Hers says *Vesper adest* ("Nigh is the Night Star"). Mine reads *Palam quod cupis capis* ("Outward you win what inwardly you want").

Index

Louis, Joe, 131
Low, David, 152, 179
Luckett, Edith, 136
Lyles, Lenny, 63

McAlister, Elizabeth, 59, 60
McCaffrey, Neil, 150, 162–63, 177
McCourt, James, 83
Mace, inventor of, 44, 45–46
McGovern, George, 116–17, 121
Mackey, John, 63
McLaglen, Andrew, 73
McMeel, John, 52
Madison, James, 112, 114
Making a Nation (MAN), 25
Malcolm X, 19
Mandel, Marvin, 58
Manilow, Susan, 123
Manson, Charles, 62
Marchetti, Gino, 63
Marcus, Stanley, 35
Marcus Aurelius, *Meditations*, 119–20
Marshall, John, 100
Marty, Martin, 6
Marx, Karl, 1
Mary Magdalene, 76
Matz, Madeline, 73
Mayhew, Alice, 72, 116
Mean Streets (film), 80
Menander, 14
Mencken, H. L., 68
Metropolitan Opera, New York, 83, 90, 92, 93
Meyer, Frank, 153, 154, 164, 177
Miller, Zell, 29
Milton, John, 14
Mishima (film), 80
Mitchell, John N., 59
Moffo, Anna, 84
Mol, Gretchen, 78, 79

Moore, Lenny, 63
Morrison, Philip, 107
Mos Def, 134
Moses, 22
Mostel, Zero, 134
Moynihan, Daniel Patrick, 103
Mozart, Wolfgang Amadeus, *The Magic Flute*, 85
Mueller, Cookie, 63
Muggeridge, Malcolm, 153
Murder in the Cathedral (Eliot), 84
Museum of Modern Art, New York, 73
Mutscheller, Jim, 63
Myers, Dee Dee, 119

Nader, Ralph, 141
Nash, Diane, 22
National Endowment for the Humanities (NEH), 122
National Review, 2, 151, 152, 154, 156, 157–59, 165
Natural Born Killers (film), 74
Neuhaus, Richard John, 153
New American Library, 37
Newark riot, 43
New England Patriots, 65, 67
Newman, Paul, 86
New York, 109
New York City Opera, 89
New Yorker, 119
New York Giants, 63–64
New York Review of Books, 3, 71–72, 76, 107
Nietzsche, Friedrich Wilhelm, 1
Nixon, Pat, 101–2, 180
Nixon, Richard M., 12, 15, 25, 59, 92, 97–108
    author's book about, 72, 103–4, 105, 107, 164
    Checkers speech of, 104